Totally Crazy Easy
Florida Gardening

The Secret to Growing Piles of
Food in the Sunshine State

by David The Good

Totally Crazy Easy Florida Gardening:
The Secret to Growing Piles of Food in the Sunshine State
by David The Good

Published by Florida Food Forests, Inc.
Florida, USA

This book or parts thereof may not be reproduced in any form, stored in a retrieval system, or transmitted in any form by any means—electronic, mechanical, photocopy, recording, or otherwise—without prior written permission of the publisher, except as provided by United States copyright law.

Copyright © 2015 by David Goodman. All rights reserved.

Lots more info on gardening and David The Good can be found at www.thesurvivalgardener.com.

To Rick Morris,

Thanks for insisting I could pull off this whole garden writer thing.

TABLE OF CONTENTS

Introduction		vii
Chapter 1	Welcome to Florida: Do This First!	1
Chapter 2	Creating Your Florida Garden: 4 Methods	9
Chapter 3	How to Fix Florida Sand—or at Least Live with It	23
Chapter 4	Easing in to Florida Gardening	29
Chapter 5	Crops That Ensure Florida Gardening Success	33
Chapter 6	Touchy and/or Low-Yielding Vegetables	67
Chapter 7	Pest Control—or How I Learned to Stop Worrying and Love the Bugs	73
Conclusion		83
Appendix I	Recommended Florida Gardening Books	85
Appendix II	Perennial and Forest Gardening in Florida	87
Appendix III	Growing Sugar Cane	91
Appendix IV	Growing Tomatoes in Florida	95
Appendix V	Five Crops That Handle Summer Heat	99
Acknowledgments		102
About the Author		104

INTRODUCTION

More than twenty-five years ago, my parents gave me a book called *Florida Gardening* by Stan DeFrietas. I still have it. (Stan, if you're reading this, thank you!)

It was my ninth birthday, and I was already a gardening nut. Rather than rolling their eyes at my strange hobby or getting on my case for the messy little patch of anemic cucumbers, radishes, and weeds I called my garden, they encouraged me.

A few years earlier, Dad had built me my first garden: a little 8 x 8-foot raised bed in the backyard. I'd planted almost every seed I could find in Mom's pantry: dry lima beans, chick peas, kidney beans... plus whatever seeds I could buy with my allowance in the local garden center. I left tools out in the yard, shared bitter radishes with my siblings, and bugged everyone I knew who had plants. I plied cuttings and seeds from old ladies and asked endless questions.

It wasn't just my parents who encouraged me. Some time before I was given my copy of *Florida Gardening*, I remember visiting my great grandpa in upstate New York and seeing his huge garden. We picked beetles off the potato plants. (I thought we were just catching bugs and was horrified when he dumped them all into a can of kerosene and torched them!) We ate berries, talked about the soil, and enjoyed the sun. He gave me a little bag of lime for my garden along with a handful of beet seeds and told me to keep growing things.

I also had aunts and uncles who gardened. I remember visiting my aunt and uncle in Hollywood, Florida, and seeing the big broccoli they were growing behind their houses. Wow! I'd never seen broccoli growing before. It was amazing!

Another aunt who lives in Fayetteville introduced me to fresh figs for the first time. Incredible!

As a child I was well-nurtured and encouraged to pursue my interest in gardening. You may not have had that encouragement. Perhaps you grew up in an apartment or in a planned community that didn't allow gardens. Maybe your parents divorced, and your dad was too busy making ends meet to spend time fiddling around with seeds.

Maybe you're a transplant to the Sunshine State with a great and glorious gardening past that came to a screeching halt when you encountered our hot sand and voracious nematodes.

Well, I'm here to encourage you. I'll be your mentor and make sure you don't fail forever.

Look around. See all the green in Florida? There are trees, creepers, weeds, moss, and all kinds of exotic plant life everywhere.

The problem is, you haven't harnessed the right crops and methods for recreating that wild abundance in your own gardens.

You can, and I'm going to show you how in this book. Are you ready for totally crazy easy Florida gardening? I will help you. Let's get planting!

Chapter 1

WELCOME TO FLORIDA: DO THIS FIRST!

If you didn't have the blessing of growing up in Florida like I did… my condolences. Welcome to Florida. This is a great place to garden.

Yes, I hear some of you scoffing at that assertion. "Yeah, right! You should see the 20-pound rutabagas my pop used to grow in Jersey!"

Yes, I know. Florida has "bad soil!" It's "too hot!" It "has no seasons!" Whatever. If you don't like it, go back home!

Ahem. Where was I?

Ah, yes. Look, you don't need to worry about the soil, the heat, and the seasons if you decide to do a little ground work to grow the plants that actually work well here. I'm going to share those methods and plants with you in this book. Once you learn how to use a cool Florida winter to your advantage and reap great armfuls of sweet salad greens and juicy cabbages from your garden, you'll never long for a white Christmas again. Well, not much.

If you just bought a property here in Florida, it's time to do a little long-term planning. The first thing I like to do on a new piece of real estate is figure out where my trees will go.

Wait… trees? What about my annual garden?

Just wait. That's next.

Why You Should Start with Trees

Fruit and nut trees are long-term food-producing scaffolding for a homestead. Seriously, there are few investments in this world that pay for themselves as well as a fruit tree does. If you spend 25 dollars on a tree, plant it and care for it for a few years until it gets established, then for the next few generations you can reap hundreds of dollars worth of its organic produce year after year.

Planning first for the fruit trees just makes sense. After you figure out where those are going, it's time for annuals!

In the center of this state, I've found that the three easiest trees to grow are mulberries, loquats, and Japanese persimmons. After planting those, I would add some "sand pears" (Pineapple pear is my favorite variety, although Hood and Flordahome are also good), along with figs. If you want to fiddle around more, add peaches, nectarines, and apples. Jujubes are also easy, as are bananas. Another great and often overlooked fruit is borne by the Pindo palm, a beautiful cold-hardy palm with fruit that tastes like coconut, pineapple, or tropical fruit. It makes the best-tasting jelly in the world. Plant multiples of each tree, and you'll have good pollination for the trees that need it.

Citrus-growing used to be easy but is no longer, thanks to the many diseases now in this state. Citrus greening is the worst. It's great if you already have a grapefruit or orange in the yard, but I wouldn't add any more citrus until a solution to getting the viral trainwreck-in-progress under control is figured out.

If you're in the northern half of the state, try planting nut trees, such as chestnuts and pecans. In you are in the southern half of the state, try planting macadamia. If you're in a totally tropical part of Florida, plant a tropical almond tree (this tree is not related to store-bought almonds). Florida is too humid for true almonds (and pistachios), although I wouldn't be adverse to trying them and seeing what happens. Don't think you're going to get much of anything. If you do, I want to hear how you did it.

If you're on the coast in the northern half of the state, you can add some plants that would be impossible farther inland, such as starfruit, mango, jabuticaba, and sea grape. They are all good choices, although they may or may not fly. None of these will do well if temperatures fall below 32º F for more than a few hours. A south-facing wall can probably support smaller trees during freezing nights. You can espalier them for better results.

In south Florida and large parts of coastal Florida, your fruit tree options are incredible. My in-laws, for example, bought a house that had a small mango orchard planted in the front yard. The trees are now gigantic and bear incredible quantities of mangoes which bring them a little side income during mango season.

My parents have a tamarind, a canistel, an acerola cherry, and a jabuticaba tree in their front yard in Ft. Lauderdale. In the side yard they have a fig and a tropical almond. Out back there are a chocolate pudding fruit, a mango, a Key Lime, a coconut palm, multiple bananas, cattley guavas, Surinam cherries, dragon fruit cactus, a Grumichama (Brazil cherry), a starfruit, plantains, papayas, and probably a few more trees I can't remember (they're all part of The Great South Florida Food Forest Project). You'll find more on that project at www.thesurvivalgardener.com).

If you want an orchard or a food forest in South Florida, all of those trees would be excellent choices.

Right now you're probably saying, "Wait a minute, I don't even know what most of those trees *are*!?"

Don't worry about that; that's part of the fun! Consider yourself a culinary explorer! Go look up those trees online, then search them out in your local ethnic market or fruit stand. Another great place to start is by seeking out some plant lovers in your hometown garden club or rare fruit tree group. Meetup.com is a good place to find some of these folks and events. You'll find there are plenty of fruit tree enthusiasts that are more than happy to tell you about their trees, direct you to great nurseries, and maybe even share some produce with you.

Here are some options for south Florida fruit trees:

- Ackee (poisonous unless harvested at the right time)
- Cashew (a fruit *and* a nut!)
- Cinnamon (large tree and very beautiful)
- Coffee (grows into a small tree)
- Custard apple
- Jackfruit (largest fruit in the world)
- Jamaican cherry (delicious, like cotton candy caramel popcorn)
- Longan (high market value)
- Loquat (grows in north and south Florida)
- Lychee (high market value)
- Mulberries (various types of mulberries will grow from Miami to New York)
- Nutmeg (probably marginal)
- Peruvian apple cactus
- Sapodilla (yum)
- Soursop (anti-cancer)
- Tropical guava

Don't forget coconut palms! Beyond the previouly listed, there are hundreds of more tropical edible trees.

The quantity of fruit you can grow in Florida is astounding. I'd bet on at least a thousand species since the tropics are *by far* a much more productive region than the world's temperate zones.

The farther north you move in the state, the more your options dwindle; however, if you like temperate climate fruit like plums, peaches, pears, and apples, you'll have lots of fun. The colder winters allow you to grow some of these northern species, such as plums, peaches, and pears, that cannot be grown in the southern tip of the state. The transition isn't immediate, but once you have overnight lows that go below the upper 20s, your tropical trees become a hard-to-grow liability rather than good orchard fodder. Conversely, your temperate climate trees need that cold to flower and fruit.

As I wrote previously, my favorite three North/Central Florida fruit trees are mulberries (white, black, Persian, and Pakistan), Japanese persimmons (both astringent and non-astringent types—both useful on the homestead), and loquats. Finding improved loquat varieties isn't easy, but they're worth buying since they bear larger and sweeter fruit than the landscape seedling trees usually found for sale.

After those, I would add the following trees to my North Florida orchard:

- Apples (Anna, Dorsett, Tropic Sweet, Ein Shemer—not the easiest, but they work)
- Autumn Olive (Small fruits for jam or ketchup—fixes nitrogen)
- Avocado (cold-hardy types such as Lila and Mexicola; subject to early death via laurel wilt disease)
- Bananas (Raja Puri, Orinoco, Red Dwarf, Ice Cream—all survive cold)
- Black Cherry (gets tall, making it difficult to harvest, but the flavor is amazing)
- Cattley (strawberry) guava (a cold-hardy relative of tropical guava)
- Chestnut (a fast producer of sweet nuts. Get two Dunstan

types or go Chinese if you have a small yard. Chinese will also cross-pollinate with Dunstan.)
- Figs (Celeste, Brown Turkey, Texas Everbearing, and LSU Purple are great. Plant Green Ischia if the birds are stealing your fruit; they don't seem to see the green figs! Stay away from Black Mission—it doesn't seem to like the Florida climate.)
- Goumi berry (Small fruits for jam or fresh eating; they fix nitrogen)
- Japanese raisin tree (rare)
- Jujube (Chinese)
- Loquats (Finding improved loquat varieties isn't easy, but they're worth buying since they bear larger and sweeter fruit than the landscape seedling trees usually found for sale. If it's been grafted—look for the graft point low on the tree or ask the seller—or is a named cultivar, i.e. the tag says "Novack" or "Big Jim" or "Christmas" or any number of other interesting names rather than just "loquat"—it's an improved type and will usually be better than the more common seedlings.
- Nectarine (check http://edis.ifas.ufl.edu/ for varieties)
- Peaches (There are some excellent varieties that were developed by the University of Florida—you can see their website for details (http://edis.ifas.ufl.edu/). Seedling peaches grown from locally picked fruit are good. My least favorite peach is Florida King due to its high chill hour requirement and failure to fruit well in most of the state.)
- Pear (Pineapple is my favorite. Orient is a good pollinator.)
- Pecan (gets big and takes a long time but has high market value)
- Plums (UF varieties—http://edis.ifas.ufl.edu/)
- Pomegranates (Note: some spontaneously die. Don't get attached!)

- Sichuan Pepper (rare spice tree)

Among these trees there are many cultivars and variations that should keep you quite contented as you plan. I currently prefer a food forest to an orchard; however, an orchard is better than having just a couple of trees... and a couple of trees are still better than a lawn. (Note: Pick up my book *Create Your Own Florida Food Forest* for lots more on food forests and species for the great state of Florida!)

As you plant, I recommend mixing up the species rather than keeping them together in blocks of the same type. That makes it harder for pests to jump from tree to tree. Running chickens through the orchard on a regular basis also feeds the trees and knocks back potential pest problems.

Along with these trees, you can add a couple of wires for grapes as a nice upgrade. Muscadines are the only grapes that do well in Florida. Stay away from champagne grapes, seedless grapes, wine grapes, etc. They'll all die from a malady called Pierce's Disease. Trust me, it's not worth it. Fortunately, there are lots of good muscadine cultivars, and they're very easy to grow.

Chapter 2

CREATING YOUR FLORIDA GARDEN—FOUR METHODS

There are as many methods of gardening as broke poets in coffee houses.

I know folks that swear by the old RoundUp, tiller, and 10-10-10 method. Of course, that makes organic gardeners want to swear as well.

But—scorched earth aside—there are a lot of different organic angles you can take. Each has its vocal defenders and attackers. You can grow in straw bales, buckets, hydroponic beds, aquaponic systems, gutters, wicking beds, traditionally spaced and hoed garden plots, vertical towers, raised beds, tires, holes ripped in bags of potting soil, 55-gallon drums... and each of those methods have their fanatical adherents. Many of them work quite well.

However, when it comes to intensive small-scale backyard production, three major gardening schools pop up again and again. These are the Biointensive method, the Ruth Stout/*Lasagna Gardening*/Back to Eden approach and Mel Bartholemew's *Square Foot Garden*. They each have their ups and downs, but all are worth trying.

Let's take a look at the following first, then continue by looking at easy container gardening for those who rent property, live in condos, or just plain stuck in small spaces.

Gardening Method #1: Biointensive Gardening

The biointensive approach is perfect for getting a productive garden going on the cheap. In fact, it's been used in Kenya and elsewhere for that very reason. Based on the pioneering work of English master gardener Alan Chadwick and improved upon by John Jeavons, this method relies on double-digging, compost, and close planting of veggies to keep the soil loose, fertile, and moist. John Jeavons's book *How To Grow More Vegetables* is a wealth of information.

One point Jeavons emphasizes—and that most gardening methods miss—is the traditional garden's need for constant inputs from elsewhere in the form of soil amendments and fertilizer. The biointensive method's answer: grow your own! Rather than telling you to "buy this" and "amend with this," he encourages you to cultivate plenty of dual-purpose crops that can be used for compost and food. Good examples include fava beans, corn, sunflowers, peas, and rye. You eat the edible parts and compost the rest.

In a time where soil loss and dependence on petroleum-derived fertilizers are front and center issues, Jeavons's approach is a breath of fresh, sustainable air.

Get started with a biointensive bed. First, dig up the weeds from a patch of ground at least five feet wide and as long as you like. Carefully toss aside nutsedge weed roots, rocks, old boots, cans, and other debris. Then double dig the entire patch with a shovel and spading fork. Add compost as you go. Blood meal, kelp meal, and manure (except equine) are also good additions though not required.

Haven't double-dug before? Well, you're in for a good workout. To double-dig your garden, make a foot-deep trench across its width, and put the dirt aside or in a wheelbarrow. Then loosen the dirt beneath with a spading fork, or turn it over with your shovel to the depth of another twelve inches or so. After that, dig up the next five-foot-wide strip and turn it into the first one as you go, continuing to dig and loosen to a depth of twenty-four inches all the way until you get to the last row. At that last row, dump in the extra dirt from the first one, and voilá—you have a beautiful loose patch of soil, all ready for seeds or transplants.

With proper double-digging, the patch ends up about six inches higher than the ground around it. The fluffiness and tilth beats the living daylights out of anything you can do with a rototiller. After this work, don't step on it! Avoiding soil compaction is key to higher yields. When roots grow easily, plants thrive.

Once your bed is prepped (which is a terrible amount of work, 'tis true), go ahead and plant it. You'll use plantings that are significantly tighter than those of a traditional garden and go for a honeycomb/triangular grid, rather than square or rectangular spacing in order to pack in the most plants possible. With frequent watering and weeding, this is a good high yield way to garden. When I tried it in my Marion County garden, I was quite pleased with the results, especially since I wasn't sure how well double-digging would work in my sandy yard. Six months after I dug the beds and three months after I harvested them, the soil, though weedy, is still fluffy and loose.

It works!

OVERVIEW OF THE BIOINTENSIVE GARDEN

Cost: Low

Prep-work Required: High

Maintenance Required: High

Inputs needed: Moderate

Yield: High

Resources:

How To Grow More Vegetables by John Jeavons
www.growbiointensive.org

Now let's take a look at the provocative "no work" gardening method of Ruth Stout.

Deep Mulch Gardening

The late Ruth Stout popularized deep mulch gardening with her highly entertaining books and columns. She called it "no-work" gardening.

The key to the "no-work" garden is mulch. Lots and lots of mulch. This is the way Ruth Stout created her rich and productive vegetable garden, and it is effective. Her book *Gardening Without Work: for the Aging, the Busy & the Indolent* has been a cult classic since the 1950s, and the method has come into new popularity recently thanks to author Patricia Lanza and her book *Lasagna Gardening: A New Layering System for Bountiful Gardens: No Digging, No Tilling, No Weeding,* No Kidding! The recent inspiring film (www.backtoedenfilm.com) also features a variant of this method as used by farmer Paul Gautschi.

The deep mulch garden uses layers of mulch to crush weeds, keep the soil moist, and add organic matter. If you're gardening on clay, it also has a major loosening effect over time. Stout's preferred mulch was straw—rotten or fresh, but she advocated using whatever organic matter that could be scavenged.

And therein lies the toughest part of this method: scrounging for materials. Getting lots of wood chips, straw, stable bedding (not equine), leaves, pine needles, or other mulching materials isn't always easy. If you don't own a truck and don't have friend with large farms or livestock, finding enough material to cover a large garden is a pain. You don't want to just put down an inch or two of mulch, either. You want to put down a foot! When you do that, the weeds don't have a chance. With sandy soils like many of us face in North and Central Florida, the addition of lots of organic material also adds a lot of fertility and life to your dirt—so don't skimp!

Here's an example of what organic matter can do: I had a few red oak trees removed from my yard a few years ago. When the men from the tree company took them down, they chopped up the trunks and larger branches and started raking great big piles of smaller sticks and leaves together. That gave me an idea. Why not pile those in a corner of my yard and let them compost? The tree crew happily obliged, and we stacked them up. The next spring, the debris had settled. Curious to see what the ground was like beneath, I started digging. What had formerly been dead gray sand was now a rich, black loam, filled with earthworms and soil life. That dirt is now some of the best in my yard. No tilling, no fertilizing or adding of amendments. Just a big stack of organic matter left to rot in place, and I was looking at grade-A soil.

Imagine doing the same in your garden plot. I've done it multiple times now, and I can assure you that the results are impressive. If you've got bad soil, sandy soil, or even clay, a deep layer of mulch will fix it.

That said—are you ready to create a patch of your very own? If you start now, you'll have a good jump on spring.

First, pick your garden plot and mark out the edges. If it's full of tall grass or weeds, mow it down, leave the clippings in place, and water thoroughly. You want it wet before you cover the ground with mulch. Next, get yourself a bunch of cardboard or newspaper and cover the entire space, overlapping to make sure nothing comes through. The same applies to newspaper: a nice thick layer is best. Though some will say you can get away with a single layer of cardboard or roughly six sheets of newspaper, two or three times that is better. Some of our Florida weeds are hard to crush.

After this weed-block layer is down, wet it thoroughly, and start adding mulch. A good mix is best. Basically, you're composting in place, so if you can mix grass clippings with pine bark, straw with manure, leaves with coffee grounds, etc., things will break down better. But the main thing is: stack it high with whatever you can get—and water as you go.

If you want to plant right away, you can pull back some of the mulch, add pockets of compost, then plant seeds or transplants. The best results, however, come a year or so after you've established your garden patch. By that point, the cardboard has rotted away, and you've hopefully added mulch on top a few more times as the previous layers have settled. The ground beneath is now full of life and compost… and your plants are strong and healthy from the abundance of moisture in the soil. See some weeds that managed to peek through? Throw yesterday's bad news on them or suffocate them with mulch. Once you've done the groundwork, the deep mulch garden is a joy to maintain. (Just don't ever till it under, or you'll undo all your hard work!)

Warning: If you've read my book *Compost Everything: The Good Guide to Extreme Composting*, you know that hay, manure, and straw are now often contaminated with garden-wrecking long term herbicides. Pick up the book for more on that—or just take my advice right here and *trust nothing*! I've had horrible experiences with destroyed plants and come across many, many gardeners who have also had their hard work destroyed with a load of hay or manure. Deep mulch gardening wasn't nearly so dangerous back when Ruth Stout was alive... now it's a minefield. It works great, so long as you don't inadvertently *kill everything* with a load of an aminopyralid-laced soil amendment.

OVERVIEW OF THE DEEP MULCH GARDEN

Cost: Moderate to high (if mulch purchased)

Prep-work required: Moderate

Maintenance required: Low

Inputs needed: High

Yield: High

Resources:
Gardening Without Work: For the Aging, the Busy & the Indolent by Ruth Stout
Lasagna Gardening: A New Layering System for Bountiful Gardens by Patricia Lanza
The Back to Eden film (www.backtoedenfilm.com)

SQUARE FOOT GARDENING

Now let's look at what may be the most popular gardening method in the U.S., the "Square Foot Garden."

The Square Foot Garden

What happens when an engineer starts gardening? The world's oldest profession gets a serious makeover! (C'mon... no, not *that* profession. Remember the Garden of Eden? Get your mind out of the gutter!)

Retired engineer-turned-gardener Mel Bartholomew's book *Square Foot Gardening* consistently tops the list of best-selling gardening books—and there's a reason. *Square Foot Gardening* promises little or no weeding, consistent results, and lots of organic veggies from a tiny space. It's not the easiest or the cheapest garden to set up—and it will drive free-styling gardeners nuts, but once created, it's prolific.

Rachelle Roper, of Florida's non-profit "Feed the Need Garden," uses a variation of this method, which makes sense considering their mission of feeding the hungry. Square foot gardening is low maintenance, easy to teach, and doesn't rely on local soil conditions.

Though I'm a permaculture-minded anarchist at heart, one spring years ago I created a set of square foot garden beds for my wife, Rachel. For years she watched my seed slinging and random plantings with bemused interest… but as the price of food kept rising, she became personally interested in gardening. However, she wasn't a big fan of my unorganized approach. She caught me one day and said "if I wanted a way to start gardening that was well-organized and easy to maintain, what would you recommend?" The answer was easy. I went on line and bought her a copy of *Square Foot Gardening* then said, "Have at it… I'm gonna go sling some more seeds around."

The book arrived, and it was right up her alley… so a short time later, we built the beds, bought some soil ingredients, and started planting.

Square foot gardening differs from most other gardening systems in that you don't use your native earth. Instead, you use a perfect mix (Mel's Mix) of "soil" created from one part compost, one part vermiculite, and one part peat moss. This creates a spongy, airy, rich medium for your plants. It's also weed-free, unless you start with homemade compost that wasn't "cooked" enough in a hot compost pile. (And even if you do think the pile got hot enough… watch out… lots of seeds usually manage to slip through the cracks.) One thing you may have difficulty finding is vermiculite in quantity. Check for big bags from your local feed stores and garden centers—it's out there, if you search. Just make sure you don't get the "fine" kind. it's a bit too dense for good garden soil.

The classic square foot bed is a 4 x 4-foot square constructed of anything from lumber to bricks to cinder blocks. Bartholomew also strongly recommends putting a permanent grid over the top, dividing the bed into easily manageable 1-foot squares. This is useful for crop rotation, replanting, seeding, and spacing. This grid can be made of stretched string, PVC, 1 x 2-inch lumber, or whatever you have lying around. Having a visual delineation of your plants is definitely helpful, but this part of the square foot garden design is often where gardeners diverge from the plans as laid down in Bartholomew's book. (Just remember: getting rid of the grid may lead to getting rid of the perfect soil mix which may then lead to chucking the raised bed concept which is certain to lead to slinging seeds across the yard and screaming *"anarchy!"* at the top of your lungs. Don't say I didn't warn you.)

When you build your square foot garden bed, you ideally won't be in contact with your native soil at all. The book recommends putting a barrier down at the bottom of the newly constructed bed. Weed block and cardboard both work. Or you can build the bed on top of concrete, believe it or not. Provided the box is 6-inches deep and contains "Mel's Mix," it will still produce. Something to consider if you're short on yard space and have a sunny slab or driveway handy. Just know this: Florida can be very hot and dry, and those beds are going to need lots and lots of water.

One benefit of this method is that you've created a rich weed-free planting medium, meaning you can plant at much denser rates than you would in a traditional garden. The yield is impressive to say the least. As you pull out spent crops, put in a handful of compost in the holes left behind and then plant again.

Does it work? Yes. Is it for everyone? Probably not. Some crops don't like the shallow soil mix, such as grain corn and cassava. However, if you want a solid workhorse garden that doesn't need a ton of watering and produces salad and veggies year in and year out, this is a good place to start.

My main beef is that I don't like raised bed gardens in general. Here in Florida the sand drains very quickly, and the sun is hot. As I mentioned previously, the beds will dry out very fast and require more water than beds grown at ground level. If you like the square foot gardening method, consider digging in your beds at ground level, rather than placing them on top of the soil.

Overview of the Square Foot Garden

Cost: High (for initial setup)

Prep-work required: High

Maintenance required: Low

Inputs needed: High (initially)

Yield: High

Resources:
All New Square Foot Gardening by Mel Bartholomew
Feed the Need Garden (www.feedtheneedgarden.com)

Easy Container Gardening

So… you don't have enough space for a regular garden? Then why not garden in containers!

Container gardening doesn't have to be a big deal. You don't have to buy expensive EarthBoxes™ (though they work nicely), sink a lot of money into a VertiGro™ system (those also work well), or buy expensive pots from your local big box store.

Chances are, you can probably start container gardening with things you already have laying around your house.

Sometimes you might want to container garden just so you can avoid the weeds, soil pests and sandy soil of Florida. There's no doubt that many plants like being in pots and don't like being in the ground here. That said, I always prefer to work with the native ground if I can, just because you can really grow a lot more in the ground overall than is easily practicable in containers.

I once saw an amazing U-Pick Florida blueberry patch that was grown completely in containers. Since blueberries like acid soil and will thrive in nothing but rotten pine bark, the owner had spread out professional black plastic weed barrier over the ground, then placed rows of halved 55-gallon plastic drums in rows, filled those with pine bark, and planted each one with its own blueberry bush. A few years later he was running a profitable little part-time U-pick operation. No dealing with pH issues in the soil, no dealing with weeds, and no dealing with soil pests.

Another good reason to grow plants in pots is that pots are transportable. If you want to grow something like coffee or jabuticaba in the northern half of the state, you can simply bring your potted tree inside when temperatures drop, rather than covering it with Christmas lights and sheets and praying it lives through a freeze.

I've used this method to grow pineapples, frost-tender lemon varieties, starfruit, guavas and other plants that normally wouldn't like our frosty overnight lows in the winter.

Yet another reason to garden in containers is if you're in a temporary living situation or have some Gypsy blood. For the nomad, it's easy to bring your containerized herb garden and some edible shrubs with you if you move.

My sister called me one afternoon while she and her husband were renting an apartment. At the time, they had young children. Earlier that day she had gone to a gardening talk and plant giveaway and had come home with a few tomato plants and other vegetables. She was interested in keeping them alive and growing some fresh produce for her family, yet wasn't exactly sure of the best way to do that given her limited living space and lack of a yard.

Fortunately, she had a sunny balcony. I recommended she get some five gallon buckets and plant in those. She filled them with loose potting mix—not sand—and they did great. One could even make five gallon buckets into self-watering container gardens. Just drill some holes in the bucket about three inches up from the bottom, and fill that portion with gravel or rough mulch and sticks. You then have a water reservoir! Fill the bucket the rest of the way with potting soil, and you're ready to plant.

My sister followed my advice. and it worked wonderfully. All that year her children picked fresh tomatoes and herbs from a thriving little balcony container garden.

Sources for free buckets include pizza and sub shops, house painters, and bakeries. If you have to buy them, they usually cost about four to six dollars each. Not bad, but not as good as free.

Note: If you get free buckets from a house painter, just make sure they were used for regular old latex house paint. It's pretty non-toxic stuff, and most of it is easy to wash out of a bucket. I'd avoid any buckets used for oil-based solvents or paints, obviously. (The proper term for gardening in containers that previously held toxins is "yuck," but I'm not going to use the word "yuck" because it sounds juvenile.)

Beyond buckets, you can also press various common items into service as container gardens. 55-gallon drums can be cut in half and used either lengthwise or around their waists. The plastic ones do tend to warp so as soon as you cut them and put in your drainage holes, pack them up with soil so they maintain their shape instead of getting weird and curly around the edges.

Another thought: if you're not afraid of neighbors calling code enforcement, you can garden in old gutted refrigerators, chest freezers, and dishwashers.

Yes, that's tacky as heck. But still… there's a lot of growing space there.

Bathtubs are perhaps a more eye-friendly option. I've used them mostly for water gardening, but if I had a few extra I'd probably plant them with herbs or a weird crop I was testing and didn't want to inadvertently lose to rambling Seminole pumpkin vines.

I've seen great gardens planted in horse troughs, too, though I think that would basically be impossible to move, so if you're going to do it, make sure you're not going anywhere for the next decade.

If you don't want to do the holes, gravel, and potting soil method of self-watering buckets (and I understand why—sorting out rocks to reuse the soil isn't fun), you can make self-watering container gardens from almost anything, provided one thing has holes… and the other thing is slightly smaller and can sit inside of it.

If you have a tray that holds a few inches of water, you can put it under your pot, then let water sit in there. It will soak up through the soil and get to the plant roots. Put pebbles in the tray if you're worried about mosquitoes breeding in your container garden.

You can also garden as my friend Mart does. He uses reusable cloth grocery bags as containers and sits them in a kiddie pool or along the edge of a pond. The reusable bags last a couple of years and soak up lots of water for your plants without becoming too waterlogged and anaerobic.

Buying yourself a little time away from your plants is a good thing. If you're like me, you forget to water now and again. Make a self-watering container garden, and that won't be a problem.

Finally, any old pots work well for container gardening, though I don't like anything smaller than a three gallon pot unless I'm starting seeds. The smaller the pot, the faster they dry out and the more watering your garden will need.

Chapter 3

HOW TO FIX FLORIDA SAND (OR AT LEAST LIVE WITH IT)

This is where the rubber meets the road. Soil amendments disappear in Florida sand like free donuts at a sci-fi convention. I can't tell you how many times I've heard "you can't grow anything in the sand here!"

Fortunately, that's not true.

Though Florida has patches of clay soil here and there, plus some muck soils and sandy loams… our predominant soil type is sand. And not fine sand or organic-matter-rich sand. A lot of it is what we call "sugar sand," which is coarse sand that eats up anything you add to the soil.

Very few of us are blessed with deep, rich loam containing the wide variety of nutrients a plant needs to grow and thrive, especially in Florida.

I don't worry about that, though. We're lucky to be alive, right? *And* living in the state where the rest of the country comes for its vacations! I mean… nobody deserves all that, let alone loam!

If things seem to be really whacked out on your property and even the grass and landscape plants look lousy, you might consider getting your pH tested. If the soil is too alkaline, a lot of plants fail to take up the nutrients they need. If it's too acid, your plants will have visions and do wacky things like listen to the White Album non-stop. You don't want either of these things. I got my soil tested for free at the local agricultural extension. Part was 6.5, another was 6.75. Those are acceptable numbers.

Rather than worrying too much about your pH, though, you can take a look at what's growing in your yard and tell if an area has decent soil. Is the grass thick? Are there lots of wildflowers? Is everything green? Does there seem to be a broad range of tree species growing in the woods across the street? If your yard is mostly crabgrass, white sand and prickly pear... and the lot across the street is filled with pines... there's a very good chance you're dealing with poor acid soil. If instead you have a wide variety of weeds and you see oaks, hickories, wild plums, bays, passion vine, wild grapes, basswood, etc... breathe easy. Chances are you have very good soil by Florida standards.

Of course, even if the neighboring lots have great soil, it doesn't always mean you will. Your lot may have been stripped of topsoil, compacted, filled with construction debris or used as the neighborhood motor oil dumping ground. If your house is more than a few decades old, you might have lead near the walls from flaking paint. If you have suspicions, get some more serious tests done. But again—if you don't have any reason to think someone used to run a nuclear reactor or something in your yard, just look around and observe your land and what grows there. They'll tell you if things are at least somewhat okay.

For Floridians with clay soils, be glad: clay usually has a lot of fertility in it. The problem, of course, is making it friable enough to work and drain properly. When I had my house in Tennessee I had to use a mattock to plant fruit trees! Not fun, though after a few years of work on the soil I was growing enviable produce. You can too.

Sandy soils have their own blessings. Because they drain well, you rarely have to worry about overwatering. They are also great for many root crops. Nutrients tend to wash through sand, however, so it does need regular upkeep to stay in good producing shape.

I confess: I love sand. It's easy to dig and hoe, it doesn't muck up your house or stain your clothes, and if you shut your eyes and walk through a patch barefoot, you can pretend you're on the beach.

My house was a foreclosure when we bought it. The yard was a mess of tall weeds and grass when we moved in. I chopped it down and started planting fruit trees right away, only to find that many of those trees were really slow to take off. It took me a while to realize that most of the front yard was made of poor, compacted sand. Along one side of the yard and in the backyard the soil was fine… but in the middle of the front yard where I put the first fruit trees was pretty lousy.

After improving my clay soil in Tennessee by piling up lots of rough mulch from tree companies, I figured I'd try the same thing here on my Florida sand and see what happened. I made a big mound of fresh leaves and tree debris in one corner of the yard… and a year later, the sand beneath was black, rich with organic matter and full of life.

The problem with sand, however, is that it doesn't stay that way for long. Once you uncover an area where you've piled up mulch, leaching and the sun and wind rapidly remove the humus from the soil.

The best way I've found for keeping sand happy is to keep it constantly covered with organic matter. As I mentioned in the previous section on deep mulching, this isn't always easy to do. A large garden requires a lot of mulch to keep covered. Fortunately, you can still keep the ground covered most of the time by keeping it planted with either crops or "green manures," which are plants you cultivate just to add organic matter to the soil. Some, like peanuts, peas and beans, also add additional nitrogen that the next crop can use.

In summer, I toss around seeds like a mad emperor dispensing gold to the masses: sunflowers, amaranth, cosmos, buckwheat, southern peas, and more. All will keep the ground healthy and moist and filled with organic matter. In the winter, I overseed with peas, lentils, chick peas, turnips, mustard, various brassicas, and grains like rye and winter wheat. These cover crops can provide some food, and at the end of the season or whenever you're ready to plant, they can be tilled, dug under, or cut and dropped in place as mulch around transplants.

Here's another story on improving sand: a couple of years ago, my dad and I started building a tropical food forest down in Ft. Lauderdale. The soil was light gray sand that drank water a lot.

Mom would put compost on her garden, and a couple of weeks later you'd never know she'd added anything. It was a South Florida Sahara. There's very little fertility in that sand. It's almost totally empty. We planted our trees, and gave them some chicken manure and 10-10-10 fertilizer to get them started. At the same time, we put down cardboard all around them as a weed block, then started gathering yard waste from all around the neighborhood. This was easy, since the city issued big green rolling trashcans to every homeowner designated specifically for yard waste. On trash day, we rolled bins from all down the block to the backyard food forest and piled it up. Long limbs, palm fronds, leaves—even chunks of log—we piled it up to a depth of three feet in some places. At first, the neighbor next door thought we were crazy, but within a few months the sand beneath was rapidly turning into dark soil. Later the same dirt looked like potting soil and was filled with worms. Previously, we had never seen a worm in that yard—yet they found the organic matter and made lots of little worm babies. It was glorious! I showed a handful to the neighbor, and he was stunned.

"I never knew you could do that," he said. "Seventy years old... and I'm still learning!"

A few years later the neighboring yards were still weedy patches of sun-baked sand, yet Dad's food forest was an oasis of jungle splendor. We basically built the fertility of a forest floor in fast-forward, and the plants were growing like weeds.

Feed the soil, and it will feed you. Loosen it, pile on whatever nutrients you have, grow cover crops, and be patient. It doesn't happen overnight. If you need to grow a garden right now, make manure tea or use chemical fertilizers. But if you want to build your sand up into something amazing, it will take some time; leaving it uncovered will eat your hard work rapidly.

Finally, if you go with the biointensive method of gardening, make sure you keep lots of compost on hand. You can grow a great garden in Florida sand without having tons of mulch, but it requires regular feeding with compost.

(If you want about a million ideas on composting and feeding your soil on the cheap, be sure to pick up a copy of my book *Compost Everything: The Good Guide to Extreme Composting*.)

Chapter 4

Easing in to Florida Gardening

There are few things more discouraging than jumping into an exciting new venture... and then being beaten back. With your garden it might be the bugs... it might be a late frost... it might be the soil... or it might be your own lack of time or just plain over-ambition at the project's start.

In times past I had grand and glorious garden plans that I put into execution only to be run over by cutworms, poor growth, lousy yields, drought, etc.

Creating solid and productive gardens usually doesn't happen right away. Practice makes perfect. Starting on a grand scale and hoping to put away piles of produce at the end of the year *will* discourage you.

I usually tell folks to start by growing their own salads, herbs, or both. If you can keep a few pots of salad greens going... and a bit of basil for the tomato sauce. you're officially gardening. If a new gardener tries to grow a ton at once, he gets burned out. He'll scrimp on soil amendments. He'll be stretching compost and not managing anything well. If you can manage a four-by-four-foot patch really well, you'll probably get more out of that than you would with a badly managed four-by-forty-foot patch.

Put serious, loving care into a small space, watch it daily, fertilize it with good stuff like kelp meal and compost, and you'll start to build confidence and the skills you need to manage a serious garden.

That little space also lets you fail small so you don't fail big later on. Some things are made to grow here. Hot peppers, for instance. They love the heat, they love the sand, and they produce like crazy—sometimes for years, provided a freeze doesn't take them out.

Most squash don't like the humidity: rot city. Onions don't like the heat and weird rain cycles. Radishes are the same. Grow them early in the early spring or plant them in the late fall. Otherwise: kaput!

Green beans usually do all right here, depending on the variety (bush beans are best). Northern pole beans often aren't happy. Snake beans, on the other hand, are almost unkillable. We'll talk more on all these crops in the next chapter, and I'll introduce you to the plants that will thrive almost no matter what.

You find these things out by planting and experimenting. I've been doing it for years. You also find out what gardening methods work the best with your personality and schedule. Spending a thousand dollars on raised beds and mushroom compost only to find that a simple row garden in the sand and a few handfuls of fertilizer work better… well, that hurts!

One problem many new Florida gardeners also face is a problem of timing. If you plant a garden in May or June like you did up north, you're not going to do well. Cabbages rarely do well after April… and beets in the late spring? Forget it!

The University of Florida has garden planting dates for spring and fall online. Look it up, and make sure you're ready to start your plot at the right time. Florida gardening is mostly divided between spring and fall plantings, with planting gaps in the dead of winter and the scorching heat of summer (except if you live in the southern part of the state where you can plant all winter and get good germination rates in the mild weather).

Now that you have set aside a little space, it's time to talk about what grows really well in Florida.

Chapter 5

THE CROPS THAT ENSURE FLORIDA GARDENING SUCCESS

There are crops that are really easy to grow in Florida. Fortunately, I've done the ground work for you on which plants grow well here. For years we've tested everything from heirloom corn to radishes and beets to kohlrabi… and tested a lot of plants you've probably never seen before, like chaya, katuk, Chinese water chestnuts, longevity spinach and more. Some have done well, some great. Some have been too much work and others were so little work that we could basically plant seeds and walk away.

My research is your gain!

If you grow the plants in this chapter, you *will* have success with your Florida garden.

Because a garden is primarily planted to feed the gardener, my focus is first on roots, then greens, then other interesting vegetables.

Pick a few that look good, then plant away!

TOTALLY CRAZY EASY ROOT CROPS FOR FLORIDA

Cassava

Inside the U.S., cassava is generally unknown except among various ethnic minorities. This root is where tapioca comes from (or "fish eyes," as my Uncle Stuart calls them) and has been used as a source of laundry starch.

The roots are really high in starch, making it a calorie-dense food. Cassava's roots contain roughly twice the calories of a comparable serving of potatoes.

Growing to about twelve feet tall, the cassava plant looks very tropical. Its palmate leaves and graceful cane-like branches are attractive in the landscape or in the garden. Cassava's pseudonyms include yuca (with one "c," not two—"yucca" is a completely unrelated species), manioc, the tapioca plant, and manihot. Whatever you call it, it's a serious staple crop. Virtually pest-free, drought tolerant, loaded with calories, capable of good growth in poor soil, cassava is a must-have anywhere it can grow. Once it hits maturity, you can basically harvest it at any point for a few years (though the roots may sometimes get too woody to eat).

But there is a caveat on cultivation: cassava doesn't like cold at all.

If temperatures drop to freezing, your cassava will freeze to the ground. This won't usually kill the plant, but it does mean you need to plan your growing accordingly.

In the tropics, cassava is a perennial, capable of growing huge roots and living for years. Here in Florida the plant does well until you get north of zone 10, where the occasional frosts will knock it down. Growing it at any zone beyond 8 is likely an exercise in futility. Cassava needs warm days and nights to make good roots. Bonus: they're easier to grow.

Of course, there is the cyanide to consider.

Cyanide?

What—you didn't think a plant this awesome could exist without a down side, did you? Yes—cyanide. The plant is full of it, from its lovely leaves to its tasty roots. Fortunately, boiling or fermenting gets it out, so fear not. A lot of plants we eat are poisonous. Just google "cashew tree" or look up the toxicity of dry kidney beans. Now *that's* scary.

Compared to many things we eat, cassava's pretty tame. Microwaveable burritos, for instance.

Now, moving beyond the cyanide—how do you grow these things? Unlike many plants, cassava is not usually grown from seeds except for breeding purposes. The only way most folks grow it is via stem cuttings. (Roots from the grocery store almost definitely won't work since they've been separated from the stem and dipped in wax.)

To grow from fresh cuttings, chop a sturdy stem into pieces about one and a half-foot long, stick them in the ground on their sides about two inches down and cover them lightly with soil, or, as I plant them, stuck in vertically with the growth buds pointing up. Within a week or so they'll be growing new leaves. Six to twelve months later (depending on care and rainfall), they'll be ready to harvest. To harvest, machete down the entire plant a foot or so from the ground, throw the branches to the side, and start digging.

Be careful, though—the roots are easy to chop through. Some careful exploratory digging

with a trowel is often a good idea. The roots you're looking for grow down and away from the main stem and are generally located in the first one to two feet of soil. They're deep brown with flaky skin. Don't dig them too long before you plan to process them, as cassava doesn't store well at all. Once you harvest the roots, you'll want to chop up the rest of the plant to make a new set of canes for planting out. I snap off all the leaves and compost them (though they can be used as a nutrient-rich cooked leafy green, I find the texture a bit too papery for my liking), then cut the bare canes into planting size.

Canes that are too green tend to rot rather than root, so throw them on the compost too.

Sturdy, one-inch plus diameter canes are perfect for planting. Plant twelve- to twenty-inch segments of cane about half their length or so into the ground and stand back so the new growth doesn't knock you over. Just don't plant them upside-down. Ensure they're right side up by looking for the tiny little growth buds by the leaf bases (or where the leaves were before they hit the compost bin). That little dot should be above the leaf's base, not below.

As for preparing the roots for the table, look them up online—there's a lot of info there.

If you live where it freezes and want to save planting material for next spring, cut long canes, and bury them in a box beneath the ground for the winter. Or you can let your current plants freeze to the ground and just wait for spring to bring new growth back.

You can also put cuttings in pots and bring them inside on freezing nights, then plant out in spring… or you can get a greenhouse and always keep a few plants in there for propagative stock. It's pretty tough stuff.

As for the work involved with this plant, it's totally minimal. The worst part is the harvesting. View it like digging for treasure, and it's fun.

Daikon Radishes

Daikon radishes, as well as their more diminutive cousin, the icicle radish, are very easy to grow. Direct seed them in early fall through about February for crops. If you plant later than that they will bolt to the sky and make lots of blooms rather than roots.

I planted a bunch of daikons this spring just because I wanted huge radishes. They're not my favorite vegetable for the table, but I love them in homemade kimchi. Easy, care-free and productive, daikons are one of those crops that succeed in Florida with very little help.

Ginger

When I was a kid, we were friends with a Chinese-Malaysian architect. He was the first person I'd ever seen growing ginger. Before I saw him pulling roots from a large flowerpot, I had no idea that ginger even was a root. I only knew it as a the zippy half of "ginger ale."

Now that I'm older, I've really come to appreciate ginger both as an ornamental and a culinary plant. Over the years, I've planted ginger root from the store many times; however, good roots are getting harder to find. A lot of what I've seen lately is limp stuff from China without any good "eyes" on it. You have to look hard to get good pieces.

You want pieces that have eyes that look like nice, healthy yellow-green bumps. That is where your new ginger plants will grow from.

When you have your nice, healthy pieces of ginger, break them up into a few pieces if they're huge chunks, and ensure each piece has at least one or two growing buds.

Bury them about four to six inches deep and wait. In a few months, ginger plants will pop up in a lovely row, and it's off to the races.

Ginger is a perennial plant, not an annual, so once you have a patch, you'll have it for years. Unlike most garden vegetables, however, ginger hates direct sunlight. Only plant it in the shade.

If you have a piece of your yard that doesn't get enough sun for regular veggies, plant it with ginger.

Ginger goes dormant in the winter, dying back to the ground. This doesn't mean it's dead. Just wait—it'll come back in late spring.

After your ginger plants have been in the ground for a year, you can pull a little of the roots, However, I find that the best harvests come at the two year mark and beyond. Dig around the base of the plant when it dies back in the fall or winter and take what you need. Just make sure you leave some pieces there to grow back the next spring.

We use ginger for seasoning (the leaves can be added to soups like bay leaves) and to treat upset stomachs (ginger is a champion at calming queasiness). I plop chunks of it into tea all through campaign season).

Malanga

Malanga is a tasty little root from the tropics. The plants are a close relative of the ornamental elephant ears used in landscaping, and they look much the same, though a little smaller.

The central roots and the side roots are edible—just toss a good bulb back in the ground when you harvest. and you'll have more the next year. The leaves are also edible when well-cooked. Look up "callaloo soup" for recipes.

Malanga is a bunching perennial that is easy to grow and divide. They enjoy a lot of water and can even grow right in ponds without rotting.

If you're interested in growing malanga, go to your local ethnic market and buy some good-looking roots, then plant them. That's how I got mine, and I've now had them growing for years.

The Crops That Ensure Florida Gardening Success

Sweet Potatoes

What makes the sweet potato easy to grow is its incredible vitality and resilience. Those vines ramble and root like nobody's business!

Sweet potatoes are one of my top crops and a staple of my family's diet. It is widely grown as an annual across the south—it's a perennial here in Florida.

A relative of the morning glory, the sweet potato is highly nutritious, calorie-filled, packs less of a glycemic hit than grains, cassava, or potatoes, and stores excellently. However, it doesn't like frost, so you're not going to get any growth during the winter. And don't plant them too early the first year—it's better to wait until there's absolutely no chance of freezing your tender young starts. If you're in the non-freezing part of Florida, plant them whenever you like.

Have you ever stuck a few toothpicks into a sweet potato from the store, suspended it in a glass, then watched the buds turn into vines? If not, grab a sweet potato and try it. The new vines that form can be broken off and planted in the ground once they get a couple of inches long. The potato will continue producing new ones for months. These little vines are called "slips." Make sure to keep them watered and shaded as they get established. Once they're established, they'll grow like weeds. You can also start slips by burying a few sweet potatoes in a planting flat or a pot and letting them grow, then breaking off the resulting vines and planting them in your garden.

I know people will tell you all kinds of things about harvest times, etc., but I usually pull sweet potatoes in November… or when I get tired of their vines covering everything. I follow the vines and pull up all I can. Invariably I've left some in the ground that return the next year, and that's fine—though yields often drop due to soil pests showing up and chewing sweet potatoes planted in the same area year after year.

One thing I discovered when I first started growing sweet potatoes seriously is that the tubers are pretty bland until you let them sit and age for a while. When you dig the potatoes, let them sit out for a little while to dry, then put them in a basket, dirty or not. After a few weeks' storage they'll sweeten up. They keep for a long time under cool dry conditions, too. I've stored sweet potatoes for over three months... and even up to six... and still had decent roots to eat, despite what you read about short storage times.

Another benefit to the sweet potato: its leaves are edible raw or cooked. We eat sweet potato leaves in our salads all summer and fall. They don't have a lot of flavor, but they're a great salad stuffer and have a pleasant crunchy texture, provided you don't pick when they've been wilted by the sun. They also fill in excellently for spinach in cooked dishes.

This plant is excellent all around—just don't eat the roots raw. They won't kill you, but they do have some anti-nutrients that are removed during cooking.

Turnips

Turnips aren't tantalizing. They're downright pedestrian and often overlooked. I've grown them off and on for years, just because I like the way they grow and because they're very productive. They used to be a complete mystery to me... and not really something I enjoyed.

Fortunately, my wife has learned to cook them in interesting ways. One time she sautéed them in butter with pork loin. That was great. The turnip pie was not.

Peeling helps take away the bitterness of turnips, as does growing them quickly with good moisture.

Reasons to grow turnips are multiple. First of all, they're very good for you—and second of all, they're also very easy to grow. They can be used to fatten hogs, they grow in the winter, they keep the ground covered, and they look pretty. Additionally, they store well, can be harvested over a decent length of season, and the greens are a good vegetable all on their own. You can also use them as baseballs or throw them through the windows of Goldman Sachs executives.

Some turnip varieties are grown solely for their leaves. If you'd like roots make sure you didn't buy seed for those cultivars. The roots of the "leaf" varieties of turnips are woody and worthless.

I plant my turnips in the late fall via broadcasting them over disturbed soil. I then rake and water them in. If you're planting a small space, just plant the seeds at a nice spacing. I prefer chucking them, of course, but you may have other, more neurotic, preferences. They come up in a week or so and grow rapidly. I tend to be able to pull my first turnips in perhaps two months or so. The harvest doesn't usually happen all at once. I usually get a few early monsters, followed by a stream of turnips hitting harvest size for weeks and weeks after that. Turnips do not like the heat, so don't plant them too late!

Yams

Yams are *not* sweet potatoes. Sweet potatoes are *not* yams. Don't get confused!

Yams are a root crop with vines that like to climb aggressively up anything they can wrap around. The naughtiest yam is *Dioscorea bulbifera*, known colorfully as the "air potato." The University of Florida hates this thing and considers it one of the worst invasive plants in Florida. Foragers aren't very fond of it either, since only some cultivars are edible and many of the wild ones kicking around the state are not. They'll usually mess you up if you eat them, so stay away. Side effects range from vomiting to sterility. Not fun, unless you're into that sort of thing. There are safe edible cultivars of *Dioscorea bulbifera* but finding them is very difficult, particularly due to the invasive plant restrictions placed on nurseries. Don't ask a nurseryman to find one for you—you'll freak him out and he'll wonder if you're trying to get him in trouble with the law. You might have luck talking to local permaculture practitioners; however, you're really not supposed to be growing this thing so I recommend leaving it alone.

That said, *Dioscorea bulbifera* has cousins with tasty roots, such as *Dioscorea alata* (the "winged yam"), "name" (pronounced "nah-may") yams (which you'll find at ethnic markets and often at Publix), Chinese yams and more.

Some of the true yams are so easy to grow that they basically need nothing except for a stout trellis or a tall tree to climb. If you harvest the roots the first year, they'll usually be pretty small, say 3–4 lbs. The second year, however, many of the yams will get huge. I have a photo on www.TheSurvivalGardener.com of a 27-lb. monster I discovered growing beneath a dogwood tree.

Yams can be grown from cuttings, from bulbils (the hanging "air potatoes," which are basically airborne roots) and from smaller chunks of a larger root buried in the spring or summer. They go dormant in the winter and die to the ground, only to re-emerge with great vigor the next spring. If they don't come up really fast in the spring, don't worry. Some wait a long time until it's good and hot to pop back up. Just wait. These babies are hard to kill.

The Crops That Ensure Florida Gardening Success

If I were to pick one root on which to survive in Florida, I'd pick the true yam. They're very, very easy to grow and quite productive with basically no input.

Totally Crazy Easy Greens for Florida

Chaya

Greens aren't all that interesting to me. That doesn't mean I cut them out of my life… but they're not as exciting as big piles of roots or amazing homemade grits. Some greens are better than others, of course.

Moringa leaves are good in soups. Spanish needle (*Bidens alba*) greens are fine in stir-fries… and turnip greens are about as interesting to me as the 1974 Estonian Women's Bowling Championships.

Yet there is a green I find quite enjoyable. So good, in fact, that I will sometimes cook up a pot and eat them as a meal. That green is chaya. I think the flavor is similar to a mild and sweet broccoli. It also has a nice chewiness to the cooked leaves I find enjoyable.

Chaya is in the same wild, wonderful, beautiful and often toxic family as cassava. It also contains some cyanide, so you need to take care not to eat it raw.

Boil leaves for at least 10 minutes, then enjoy them. They're ridiculously good for you and full of vitamins, which makes sense to me since they taste hearty and delicious.

Growing chaya in Florida is a cinch if you can find cuttings or a rooted plant at a rare edible nursery. Cuttings root in a month or so when it's warm. Just stick them in moist soil and wait. They're not as fast as cassava but they'll usually take.

I've seen chaya wild down in South Florida, but in the northern half of the state you're not likely to come across it. Where I live it freezes to the ground every winter but will usually return from the roots and rapidly shoot for the sky. Once you get a couple plants, it's easy to make more.

Bugs don't usually bother my chaya plants (*cyanide*!) and they grow decently even in poor soil. I've planted them in full sun and in almost full shade and they've lived in both places, though the ones grown in shade are thin and leggy.

Grab some chaya, tuck a few into your yard... and you'll have great perennial greens for years to come. This plant's a winner.

Collards

If you're in Florida and you're not growing collards... what's wrong with you? Collards are an under-appreciated staple of the Deep South. When it's collard season, it's really collard season down here. Piles of them overflow from the back of pickup trucks by the side of the road—and if you're interested in growing lots of food for very little work, that's just what you want. Overabundance.

The thing that really makes collards key down here is their season. In the northern half of the state, many other crops get toasted by frost... but not these guys. They'll feed you right through the winter when your other plants are long-gone. You can stuff your freezer with these without much trouble. One year I put away about forty pounds of collards and we ate them all year. We even dried some to add to soups and omelets. Out of the brassica family, collards are right up there with radishes on the "ease of growing" scale. They're tough, take the cold, grow and grow and grow, and rarely if ever will fail to give you a harvest.

Other bonuses to collards: young leaves are excellent in salads. Cooked and cut in strips, collards can also fill in for pasta in low-carb diets. (Rachel The Good makes a killer "collard lasagna.") They can also be used to threaten children, as in "Clean your room or so help me I'm gonna serve collards again tonight!"

To plant the easy way, prepare a bare patch of ground, then scatter seeds, rake them around, and water for a week. Baby plants will come up everywhere. Thin as needed to give them space for growth and eat the thinnings. Harvest leaves as needed—the plants will take a lot of cutting.

And seriously—if you're not growing these yet, set aside a patch. Spring or fall: collards are a must-have.

Edible-leafed Hibiscus and their Kin

When you think of delicious homegrown salad greens, you probably think of lettuce or spinach or mustard—not hibiscus! Hibiscus is just that big flower that decorates Hawaiian shirts.

Vegetables aren't normally printed on shirts, right?

The strange truth is that many Southerners already eat a very controversial hibiscus known as "okra." We'll look at that a little later—but suffice it to say that there are a lot of edible species of hibiscus and hibiscus cousins (such as Jamaican sorrel, which we'll also cover later). The great thing about these hibiscus—they're perennial! Plant them in a permanent bed or in your landscaping and you'll be harvesting them for years, unless the iguanas beat you to it.

One of my favorite salad greens for Florida is *Abelmoschus manihot* (formerly known as *Hibiscus manihot*). This great plant makes huge green leaves the size of dinner plates, though it rarely flowers. Finding this species is hard, though you may have luck if you visit ECHO in Ft. Myers.

Another hibiscus that's edible and easy to grow is the "Turk's cap" or "sleeping hibiscus." It features hanging blooms which are edible, though the leaves are too coarse to be worth eating (they do make good rabbit or goat feed, however). The tropical hibiscus plants often sold in garden centers also have edible blooms. Add them to salads for a splash of color.

One more hibiscus that's a great little green is the deliciously tart cranberry hibiscus, known properly in Latin as *Hibiscus acetosella*. This plant is sometimes mixed up with Jamaican sorrel, though its leaves are a dark maroon color and the calyxes on the flowers aren't worth harvesting like the Jamaican sorrel's calyxes are. It's also a true perennial, growing year after year and bearing lots of tart leaves that make a bright and tasty addition to salads. To me, they almost taste like Caesar dressing—zippy! This hibiscus will grow all the way through the state and is moderately cold-hardy, though it will usually get some frost-damage during winters north of Orlando. Don't worry if it does—it'll almost always sail through and produce again.

Kale

Roughly 2400 years ago, Hippocrates wrote "Let food be thy medicine and medicine be thy food." I've got a gut suspicion he was thinking about kale when he wrote that. There are reports of kale helping reverse the progression of Multiple Sclerosis, lower cholesterol, improve eyesight and fight cancer. Kale is believed to contain the most nutrition per calorie of any known plant. That should be reason enough to grow it!

Kale is a cool-season biennial that's among the easiest of garden plants. It thrives on double-dug beds, even in sand, and can produce for more than half the year. Plant kale in fall or early spring, taking care not to bury the tiny seeds too deep. One kale plant (depending on variety) can easily grow a couple of feet tall and spread to the same extent. I over-seed, then eat what I thin out. Give them enough water when they're little and they'll reward you with plenty of growth.

Unlike tomatoes and other warm-season crops, kale isn't fazed by frosts. The taste gets even sweeter after a frost. In Florida, kale grows all the way through the winter; further north in the state its growth may slow or stop if it's cold. If you're a gourmet, consider growing the attractive "Lacinato," or "Dinosaur" kale.

The only time it's hard to grow kale is in summer. High temperatures are kale's enemy. The season could likely be expanded if you grow it under grape trellises or taller crops so it's protected from the worst of the sun's heat. Of course, even if your kale does give up, it's going to be at a time when you're likely to have plenty of other warm-season veggies to enjoy.

Next time you see a spread of hors d'oerves on a bed of deep green... skip the cocktail wieners and eat the kale. Your body will thank you (even if the hostess looks at you sideways).

You get extra points for growing the kale yourself.

Lettuce

Why would you buy lettuce when growing it in Florida is so *easy*? Probably because you didn't have this book to set you straight.

If you like lettuce, you're in luck. Here in Florida it doesn't make sense to grow picky iceberg lettuces, but leaf lettuces are ridiculously easy to pull off during the cool season.

I plant lettuces by weeding and clearing a bed, then raking it smooth. Then I take a couple of packets of lettuce seed and sprinkle them all across the surface and lightly rake them in, then water well for the next week or two until they all pop up.

For less than $4.00 you can eat a hundred salads.

That makes a lot of cents... er... sense.

Lettuce likes compost and hates the heat. Cut individual leaves off when you harvest, or slice off the entire top and let it grow back—they often will.

Longevity Spinach

Longevity spinach is a rather recent addition to my gardens. I've been cultivating it for about three years and have found it to be easy-to-grow, tasty, productive and a winner even during the heat of summer.

Longevity spinach, known in Latin as *Gynura procumbens*, is a perennial vegetable that's alleged to balance blood sugar, lower cholesterol and high blood pressure as well as increase concentration. Whether or not those secondary benefits are real, this is a very good vegetable for Florida.

To grow longevity spinach, plant cuttings in a pot out of the sun and they'll root within a few weeks. It's so easy to grow from cuttings that I've had them take just from pieces of stem I've stuck in the ground in my food forest. This plant, so far as I know, is always grown from cuttings, not seeds.

If you're in a frost-prone part of the state, grow longevity spinach in a sheltered location or make sure to keep some in a pot so you can pull it indoors during freezes. I usually start a few cuttings on a sunny windowsill in late fall before the first frost, then plant them out in the garden when all the frosts have passed.

Longevity spinach grows very rapidly when it's warm and sunny. It's half-upright, half-vining and you can increase leaf production by pruning back the shoots. Plant what you prune off, and you'll soon have even more longevity spinach to share with your friends.

Mustard

Growing mustard in Florida is easy and very satisfying.

Mustard greens are one of my favorite potherbs. This plant is easy to grow and is remarkably healthy for you—plus it contains anti-cancer compounds. Though it's not as cold-hardy as kale or collards, mustard will stand quite a bit of frost before dying. Mine have survived the mid-20s without damage. In fact, if you want success, you cannot plant these during the warm part of the year. If you do, the plants will rapidly bolt and peter out. As temperatures rise, they get all crazy and overwhelmed with the desire to make babies. Here in North Florida, I put my mustard in around the beginning of November, then harvest leaves through the winter. If you live in South Florida, plant it any time during late fall or winter. Boiled, mustard has a texture and flavor we prefer to its cousin collards. Stir-fried, it has a spicy bitterness the kids don't really like—and I agree with the kids.

From seed, mustard germinates quickly and you can start harvesting leaves in about a month. Depending on the variety, you can get purple leaves… curly leaves… or even huge leaves. I cut off leaves as I want them and the plant continually produces new ones. I can barely keep up with the 24 or so plants I have going right now.

Another benefit of mustard: mustard can kill nematodes when used as a green manure. Just till or hack your mustard plants viciously into the soil as soon as they start bolting in the spring, then plant your next crop.

Of course, if you let the plant go to seed, you can make your own delicious mustard from the resulting seeds. I might save some to try that as well one year… because in the upcoming econopocalypse, we're really going to miss having good condiments. Especially as we're forced to eat rats and gnaw on old boots for sustenance.

If you haven't done it before, set aside some space for mustard this year… it's well-worth growing.

Surinam Purslane

Surinam purslane is a cousin of the purslane "weed" that's been well-known as a healthy edible since time immemorial. It's also called waterleaf, but the best way to hunt it down is via its Latin name *Talinum fruticosum*. This is a very easy Latin name to remember. Just think of Tiny Tim's cover of "Tiptoe Through the Tulips" and sing it!

Talinum fruticosum…
In the garden
Come away with me…
Oh Talinum fruticosum… with meeeeeeee!

Okay, now that I've ruined your day with that particular earworm, let's take a closer look at Surinam purslane.

Surinam purslane is a fleshy, upright plant with leaves that can get about 3-inch long and are fleshy, though not as thick as common purslane. The young stems are crisp and edible along with the leaves. Surinam purslane also features pretty little pink blooms that open in the afternoon and develop into tiny seed capsules filled with itty-bitty seeds. The plant is a vigorous self-seeder. Though it's a tropical plant, Surinam purslane grows well in North Florida and will sometimes return from the roots after a freeze. It will also sometimes self-sow and come back in the same location after a harsh winter. In South Florida it's a great source of year-round salad greens.

Plant in full to half sun. I grow Surinam purslane via cuttings. All I do is break off a 6-inches or so piece of stem and pop it in the ground somewhere. They almost always root.

I find this plant tastes better raw than cooked. It has a crisp fleshiness with a little bit of sweetness and a tiny bit of bitter in the background, somewhat like lettuce. The leaves are a bit small to use as a staple green; however, they're a refreshing and watery snack on a hot afternoon while passing through the garden.

Turnips

I wrote on turnips as a root crop previously. To cultivate turnips for their leaves, grow them the same way, just harvest the tops as you want them. They're very healthy and are good steamed or boiled. Serve to the Estonian Women's Bowling team for extra cool points.

Water Spinach (Kangkong)

Kangkong is an oriental green and a relative of sweet potatoes. Its Latin name is *Ipomoea aquatica* and you're not going to find it in Florida nurseries due to its status in the state as an invasive plant, despite its great usefulness as a healthy and easy-to-grow vegetable.

The place you may find it, however, is in Asian markets. If you can find a fresh bundle of shoots, the stems root easily. That would be a very bad thing for you to do, however, since this is an *evil invasive species*.

If you decide to sin against the state of Florida and grow water spinach, just make sure you don't grow it near any canals or waterways where it might take off. Kangkong is a rapidly growing, vining plant that crawls along the ground or across the surface of the water and roots as it goes.

If I were to ever come in contact with this foul invasive, I imagine I'd like it lightly steamed and served as a side dish with stolen sweet potatoes and a steak purchased from obvious cattle rustlers. Since it totally can't be grown in the state of Florida where I live and therefore I can't actually have ever eaten it, I just imagine kangkong as having a wonderful earthy flavor with hints of mushroom and asparagus.

An evil cultivator of this naughty crop would pick the leaves or entire young tender shoots, which would then be steamed, boiled, added to poached manatee soup or sautéed in a dirty pan by scantily clad painted ladies in an opium den.

Finally, I've been told by criminal investigators that kangkong can't take the frost and only grows really well when it's nice and hot outside.

OTHER TOTALLY CRAZY EASY VEGETABLES

Bush Beans

Other than radishes, growing green beans is about as basic as it gets. Reliable, productive, tolerant of poor soil and tasty, they are one of the first crops any new gardener should try.

Of course, there are many, many beans that fall into the "green bean" category. If it's called a "green bean," that basically just means it's a bean with an edible pod you eat while the beans are still unripe. If it's a variety you let hang on the plant until the beans are basically ripe, it's a "shell bean." Some varieties of shell beans are eaten while still soft, others are allowed to dry completely until you have "dry beans."

Beyond the "shell" or "green" varieties, beans also come in "bush" and "pole" varieties. Bush beans are usually small, squat plants that can stand without support. Pole beans are climbers and need trellises to do well.

Of all the beans, the bush green beans are the ones that are totally crazy easy. No trellises, no drying, no shelling. Plus, quite a few can be grown in a small space.

When I was six and went to the store with Dad to buy some seeds, the first ones that really caught my eye were Burpee's "Brittle Wax" yellow green beans. We bought them… and they went into my very first garden. I'm still growing them today because they're consistent, productive and taste good. They're not the most flavorful bean we grow, but they look cool.

Another cool-looking bean that my wife really likes are the purple-podded Romano beans. The purple color makes them really easy to see and pick on the plants, even though they turn green when cooked. I originally bought seed at a big box store… and never saw them for sale since, except online. Territorial seed carries them, fortunately, and you'll find other purple-podded types for sale now and again.

Beyond varieties—let's talk about culture. Beans like warm weather and will not stand freezing temperatures. Bush beans do not have the strong root system of pole beans, so they need a bit more water to stay happy. Plant your beans 1-inch deep and about 6-inch apart in rows roughly 12-inch apart and you'll do fine. In a week or less, they'll pop up and it's off to the races.

Beans usually start producing pods in less than two months—and once pods start getting to picking size, keep them picked. If you don't, the plant will give up producing new pods. Plant a few small beds and you'll get enough to eat every day, share at church and probably freeze as well.

Bush beans can be sown multiple times through the warm season and you'll get more beans that way. Plant a new bed every three weeks or so and you'll be rolling in tasty pods.

As for pests, you'll get stink bugs and maybe bean beetles later as the summer progresses. I don't worry about them unless we get a total plague. One year the bean beetles totally chewed through a bed I'd planted. Fortunately, we'd already harvested plenty of beans. It was my own fault they went nuts, though—I had planted the bean bed in a monoculture. Nice, even rows for the beetles to feast upon… nothing but beans for miles, man.

If you get problems like that, just till the beans under, bugs and all, wait a bit, and start over again. Or burn them. Or chuck them over the fence for your chickens to mangle. No big deal. Seed is cheap and beans grow fast. Beans are also a nitrogen-fixer, so planting them in front of demanding crops and on new ground is a great way to give your garden a boost of fertility. I throw beans into empty corners during the warm season, just as I do with peas during the cool season. They're tough enough to thrive without much care... and they feed the ground? Yep. All aboard the bean train!

But... the best thing about green beans? Letting your kids eat them right out of the garden, sweet and sun-warmed. When I pick a basket, I always acquire little "helpers" who wish to eat the beans. And since the pods are pesticide-free, nutritious and abundant... who am I to say no?

Everglades Tomato

Tomatoes are generally a pain in the neck to grow in Florida. They don't like the cold and they don't like the heat. Stink bugs and leaf-footed bugs destroy them on the vine. Too much rain and they split... not enough calcium and the fruit rot. (I've dedicated Appendix IV to growing tomatoes in Florida, so if you really want to hear more of the horrifying details, skip ahead to there.)

There is, however, one excellent exception to the "tomatoes are a pain in the neck to grow in Florida" rule. That exception is the so-called Everglades tomato.

This scrappy, tiny-fruited little heirloom is remarkably sweet and rich in tomato flavor. It can become a perennial in South Florida and will often self-seed in North Florida. Though the fruit are too tiny to put on a burger like a nice slice of beefsteak, Everglades tomatoes are delicious in salads, salsas and as a snack right from the garden. The vines are sprawling and unwieldy, sometimes covering entire garden beds with their rambling branches.

In South Florida you can plant Everglades tomatoes at any time. Where it freezes, start them a few weeks before the last frost date and plant them out, or direct seed when it's warm. Grow tomatoes on top of compost and they'll do better than in regular soil.

Hot Peppers

For quite a while I wasn't much of a pepper grower, though I love spicy food. I fiddled with bell peppers, jalapeños, habeneros and other peppers to add a little spice to our kitchen but never planted many at one time until a year ago when I started a bunch of them to sell in my plant nursery.

Unfortunately, I *way* over-estimated the demand for hot pepper plants and ended up with at least a hundred various plants that didn't sell and were rapidly outgrowing their pots.

Since it was nearing the end of summer, I decided to plant a bunch of them in my garden—and we reaped lots and lots of spicy peppers until frost arrived and ended my pepper plantation.

In Florida, bell peppers rarely do all that well unless you take great care of them. Even then, they often get destroyed by insects. Hot peppers, on the other hand, were *made* for Florida! They'll keep producing in the heat and through the summer when tomatoes and almost everything else gives up. In Ft. Lauderdale I once saw a 3-year-old cayenne pepper plant that was almost as tall as me and loaded with sweet hot peppers.

Yep—that's one of the reasons hot peppers rock: they're perennial. Once you plant these guys, they'll last multiple years and keep fruiting for you as climate conditions allow. If you get a nasty frost, they'll die. I piled mulch over four plants before freezing weather one year, then uncovered them in the spring. Two came back. Grow them in big pots and you can keep them alive by hauling them inside on frosty nights.

To grow peppers, plant the seeds in flats or in the ground after the last frost date. They grow quickly and usually will bear in about three months. Interestingly, I've had them self-seed here and there around my gardens. Occasionally, I'd toss a rotten pepper aside, or throw some in the compost... and a little baby would come up. If I liked its location, I'd leave it. If not, I'll transplant them into a bed.

The only pest problems I've had with hot pepper cultivation involve stink bugs. They'll ruin a few peppers here and there by punching their nasty mouth parts into them and leaving spots that rot—yet even with those losses, we end up with plenty of peppers for the spice cabinet each year. Five plants will provide you with lots of peppers—plant more than that and you may need to start your own hot sauce brand. Something like *Smack Me on My Flaming Butt of Death and Call Me Poppa Satan 'Cause My Fiery Mouth Is in Hell*™ should sell.

For making salsa, jalapenos excel in juiciness and good raw flavor; in brutal heat and smokiness, habeneros are king. For a mild pepper for packing with cheese and rice, poblanos are tops. The cayenne's flavor is sweet and hot at the same time—and it makes amazing ground red pepper (you can see my method on my website here).

The cayenne is a pepper that's made for drying. It's got lower moisture right off the plant, so if you string them up, they'll usually dry pretty well. If you have a lot of humidity (like I do), you can stay safe from mold by putting them in a dehydrator to dry instead. I've done this with a mix of hot peppers and made some super-hot ground pepper that tastes amazing. I've also smoked the peppers, then made smoky hot sauce that tasted so good it was impossible to stop eating it. Plant hot peppers and you will have gardening success!

Jamaican Sorrel

Jamaican sorrel is one of the coolest-looking edibles you can grow. And not only is it beautiful, it's delicious. Jamaican sorrel, also known as Florida Cranberry, is a member of the hibiscus family. The blooms, leaves, and pods on this plant are all edible—but the reason most people grow Jamaican sorrel is for the calyxes.

What is a calyx, you ask? It's the pointy fleshy red bit at the base of the flower.

After blooming, the flower withers and the pod inside the bud begins to swell. After a few days, the calyx around it is large and juicy—ready for picking.

I use scissors to take them off my bushes when they're about an inch across. Chop the stem end off, slit one side and pop out the green fruit in the middle (they're like freaky little okra babies… I send them right out the door to the chickens). Then save the calyxes in the freezer until Thanksgiving—they're a dead ringer for cranberry, though not as bitter.

My wife uses them interchangeably with cranberries in her sauce making… and the results are delicious. (Check out Rachel's faux cranberry sauce recipe here.) The light cycle effects when these start their blooming, so keep that in mind. You'll have lovely flower-less bushes until sometime in October, then the blooms arrive in profusion. Pick regularly to keep the plant going, which it will until frost.

Another great thing about these plants: the leaves are delectable. They have a lemony-tart and satisfying flavor that's perfect in Caesar salads. Try it—they'll blow your mind.

You can start these guys from seed in the spring, then transplant out—or simply direct seed after the last frost date. They'll grow like crazy with a little care. We're talking 6 feet! Finding seeds may be difficult, but search anyhow. They function as both a salad green and a tart fruit. Very worth growing.

Moringa

Moringa has been called the "Miracle Tree," and for good reason.

It has an incredible assortment of attributes in its favor. From cleaning water to fending off malnutrition, it's a tree of many uses. Fast-growing, easy to grow and containing complete proteins in its leaves, the Moringa is a must-have for Florida survival gardeners. If you're stuck living off rice and MREs, you're going to want more nutrition—and that's where this tree shines. The leaves are absolutely loaded with nutrients, brought up from deep down by the tree's questing roots. The tree has been named the "most nutritious on earth." One of these days we'll have to put it in the ring with kale for a death match. Moringa is also anti-bacterial and anti-fungal, as well as being a really fast producer of biomass. Its pods are often called "drumsticks" and feature prominently in some regions of South Asia, however, it's sometimes hard to get them to set pods in regions with frost.

From seed, the Moringa will easily hit 10 feet during its first year of growth. In the tropics the tree apparently reaches 60 feet, though the wood is very weak. Some of my moringa trees blew through 20 feet in their second year.

But tall trees aren't really what you want. You want trees that are easy to harvest. To get that, simply cut the trunks at about 4 feet and let them shoot up lots of tender new growth. The compound leaf stems are easy to break off so the tiny leaflets can be dropped into soups, sprinkled into salads or dried/frozen for future use. After learning of its incredible nutrient profile, I've started putting the leaves into everything from smoothies to scrambled eggs. Bonus: they taste good when cooked.

The trouble with this tree, however, is that it's a tropical all the way. It quits growing when the weather gets cool—and freezes to the ground during a frost. That means those of us in the central to northern part of the state won't get 60 foot trees that collapse onto our roofs during thunderstorms. Fortunately, the Moringa is hard to kill and in spring will generally come back from its roots. Crop them low in South Florida and treat them like a vegetable.

Plant moringa seeds (or stick cuttings) in desired locations. Watch them shoot to the moon, and then harvest the leaves as desired. Cut back the trees to 3–4 feet, and harvest lots of new growth to dry for storage. Put a 2-foot diameter ring of chicken wire around the base of the tree, and fill with straw to protect against frost. Cut off all top growth and save the leaves, then cover the cut trunk. Wait until after all danger of frost the next year and then remove the ring and straw. *Boom!* The Moringa flies back into action as soon as the days warm up, and you'll be harvesting fresh leaves again.

The trees I protected from frost came back with significantly more vigor than those I simply let freeze to the ground. I've read that you can dig the roots and grate them to make a horseradish substitute—but I've also read that the roots are somewhat toxic. If you try it, let me know if it works out or if you suddenly die. I have yet to see any pods develop here in North Florida, though one of my protected trees has flowered. The blooms dropped, sadly, but perhaps some year we'll see some pods produced.

Okra

Think of okra as a slimy hibiscus. It's technically in its own genus, but it's still a close enough cousin that you'll recognize the blooms as kin when you see them.

With okra, the main edible portion is the green seed pods. Don't pick them too late or they're fibrous and too tough to eat easily. Once okra starts producing, it really produces!

Seek out "spineless" varieties or you'll suffer when you pick them. It's best to save the real suffering for when you actually eat this slimy veggie.

Okra leaves are also edible but not as nicely textured as some of the other members of the hibiscus clan.

Direct seed in the spring in soil that's been amended with compost. Nematodes *love* okra so don't plant it in the same place more than once. Alternating with mustard or other brassicas is also a good idea, since the nematodes hate those.

Perennial Cucumber AKA Ivy Gourd

Oh shoot. Here's another one that made the invasive species list. (Is it just me, or is there a conspiracy to find the easiest to grow vegetables and put them on the "banned" list?)

Also known as the ivy gourd—or more properly, *Coccinia grandis*, the perennial cucumber hails from India and tropical Asia and is a deliciously sweet-tart cuke that already tastes a bit like a dill pickle.

It is indeed a perennial, making a decent-sized root beneath the ground that allows it to spring back and reach for the sky after a frost.

The cucumbers are striped green and only get to be about 2–3 inches long. When they ripen, they turn red and aren't good to eat.

In some places, this plant has become a serious invasive, though there are sterile varieties that don't set viable seeds and would be very useful for home gardeners. Propagation can be attained through vine cuttings and probably through root division.

Ivy gourd is edible raw or cooked and produces buckets of little cucumbers through the warm season with little or no pest problems, unlike its more commonly cultivated annual cousins.

It's also alleged to have some health benefits… though all I know is that it's delicious. Uh, I mean, some Indian acquaintances have told me it's delicious.

Seminole Pumpkin

Unlike regular pumpkins, Seminole pumpkins thrive in Florida and are uniquely suited to the climate and bugs of the Sunshine State. Originally selected by Native American tribes before the Spanish landed, they were later named after the Seminole tribe—though those folks arrived much later in this pumpkin's history.

These pumpkins are incredible for a few reasons. First of all, Seminole pumpkins root along the nodes of the vine. Every joint where a leaf emerges will root into the ground, effectively making the plants somewhat modular.

If vine borers get into one section, the roots in the next section will still keep the plant alive, unlike many other varieties of squash which may look great one day… then be wilting the next day... then be dead two days later due to getting drilled out by nasty borers.

Seminole pumpkins also fly through the humidity that often causes downy mildew on other squashes. Try to grow Hubbard squash or nice acorn squash in Florida and you have an uphill battle. Your only hope is to plant as early as possible and pray the borers and the wilt don't get them before they produce a measly half-sized squash or two.

I've grown Seminole pumpkins in the spring and had them produce the first round of fruit by the end of June, then keep growing vines through the summer and pop out another round of pumpkins in the fall.

Seminole pumpkins have another benefit: they taste good. They make a better pumpkin pie than the tasteless pie pumpkins from up north and are good simply cut open and roasted in the oven until soft. If you're gardening in fear of the future, this is also a great pumpkin because of its extremely long storage time. I've eaten one that was still good after *two years* on the shelf!

Seminole pumpkins grow the very best on a pile of compost or in a melon pit (get my book *Compost Everything: The Good Guide to Extreme Composting* for serious info on growing vegetables with minimal compost and getting great yields!), but they'll also grow in any somewhat decent soil, though yields and vigor will be lower.

Down south I've heard it's possible for Seminole pumpkins to become a short-lived perennial; however, further north, the freezes take them out rapidly in the fall or winter.

One problem with Seminole pumpkins is the variability in genetics I've discovered as I've tested this uniquely Floridian crop. Some strains have very small fruit, ranging from 1–3 pounds...

and other strains have fruit weighing almost 15 pounds. Some vines also seem to give up quickly without bearing a lot of pumpkins—other selections will produce again into fall as I noted previously. One of my personal gardening projects has been to select good varieties and breed for yields, flavor, size and vigor.

Speaking of vigor, be careful where you plant Seminole pumpkins! They'll cover a garden bed, a fence, a tree or even your house if given half a chance. Give them lots of space or encourage them onto trellis if you so desire. Once they start growing, you can almost watch them grow.

When the stems attaching the pumpkin fruit to the stems turn yellow, it's time to harvest. Carefully nip them off with a pair of pruning shears, leaving at least an inch or so of stem on the pumpkin. This will help it keep a lot longer. Before eating, also give your pumpkins about a month on the counter or a shelf to "cure" and sweeten up, otherwise they'll taste more starchy and less delicious.

If you want an easy, tasty, long-keeping Florida heirloom that's just downright fun to grow and harvest, grow Seminole pumpkins—and if you do, please contribute photos to my ongoing Seminole pumpkin variety gallery at http://www.thesurvivalgardener.com/the-seminole-pumpkin-projec/.

Snake beans

These are the easiest beans to grow, ever. *Vigna unguiculata*, also called the yard-long bean, the snake bean, the asparagus bean and various other weird names, is a tropical Asian green bean that kicks tail in Florida. I mean, *serious* tail. This thing is a monster.

Let's talk about how crazy awesome these babies are.

The vines grow quite tall (usually around 8–12 feet) with little or no care. If you grow these, which you should, make sure you've got plenty of climbing room for them.

You can basically plant snake beans at any warm time of the year as long as you give it enough water to get started. I've planted them in midsummer and gotten a good crop, as well as in fall and spring. This sucker grows like a weed. I've even stuck seeds in the front yard and let them run across the grass and eat neighboring trees and shrubs. With zero care, they still bore beans. I once planted them in a spot that received only indirect light: they bore a good crop anyhow. Another time I planted them on a baking-hot fence. Same deal. Tons of beans.

And what beans: the taste is almost nutty. A lot of green bean flavor with undertones of roasted almond and asparagus.

Snake beans take a little while to get started. For a few weeks, they're just cute little bean plants. And then they pull the Incredible Hulk routine on you and reach for the sky in a blinding green rush.

The seeds are available rather widely now in a variety of cultivars. Every one I've grown has been productive and worth growing except for the purple-podded types. They're beautiful, but they yield less and are less tasty and more fibrous.

Bugs leave them alone for the most part (though leaf-footed bugs will cause some trouble, and occasionally aphids will show up in droves) and the vines are really, really good at climbing on whatever is handy.

This plant is also a nitrogen-fixer and a good source for compost at year's end. It has no tolerance for frost, however, so don't plant it too close to frost dates.

The beans can be eaten raw or cooked and continue bearing for a few months after maturity. Pick the pods before they get too big and leathery. You'll get a feel for it quickly when you grow them. Just a few beans are enough for a good serving at dinner.

And There You Have It!

If you plant your garden just with selections from the above list, plus a couple of loquat trees, several Japanese persimmons, a few mulberry trees, and a couple of chestnuts, you're going to have a wildly productive homestead.

Imagine a salad of freshly picked hibiscus leaves, cucumber and Surinam purslane in a vinaigrette, followed by roasted Seminole pumpkin with butter and sea salt or a baked home-grown sweet potato, a side of sautéed snake beans and some garden-fresh jalapeno and Everglades tomato salsa.

Start with these crops and you'll be eating *well!* It's not that "nothing grows in Florida"—it's that we're just not growing the right crops! Now that you have this list, get out there and start putting together a garden that will feed you with a lot less work than you ever thought possible.

Chapter 6

Touchy and/or Low-Yielding Vegetables

Since I know I'm going to get asked questions about some of the more common vegetables people like to grow, I'm going to cover some of them below. Yes, some are worth growing once you nail down the really easy stuff above... but don't count on them right at the beginning.

In Florida, I've found the following crops are either not "totally crazy easy" or they just don't produce enough for the space they take up.

Arrowroot

Arrowroot is very easy to grow and beautiful to look at, but the yields are small. Roots require extra processing. It's good as a non-recognizable background sort of survival crop if you're worried about the end of the world and someone stealing your sweet potatoes... but not really much of a staple.

Asparagus

Asparagus yields are poor, and they seem to hate our climate. They are maybe worth trying to grow only in the northern half of the state. I just pick and eat wild smilax shoots instead.

Beets

Beets can be touchy. Sometimes they grow, sometimes they don't. I grow them anyway, but they are a bit sad some years. Fortunately, the greens are also edible cooked.

Broccoli

Broccoli is really not that difficult to grow, but the heads are sometimes subject to rot or bolting. Broccoli also requires pretty good fertility. I do grow it, but it's not totally crazy easy.

Brussels sprouts

I never have had much luck with brussels sprouts down here. They require a long, cool season and rarely set great sprouts despite my best efforts. Blah.

Cabbage

Cabbage isn't that hard, bug it does require good timing and high soil fertility. If you want to grow cabbages, stick with fast-growing, smaller-headed types.

Cantaloupe

Cantaloupe is touchy; it's subject to rotting, pest damage, mildews, and getting rained on too much. It can taste way too watery.

Cucumbers

The perennial cucumbers noted previously are easy—but regular cucumbers often are bitter, misshapen, or killed by worms, etc. If you still want to grow them, I've found that pickling types seem to do better than the larger-fruited varieties.

Eggplant

Bugs love to eat eggplants. Smaller Asian types do better for me than the big fat ones.

Garlic

I spent some years in Tennessee and grew some good garlic there. In Florida I've had problems with it rotting, failing to set heads, and just randomly dying back before anything happens. That doesn't mean there aren't good types worth trying here—feel free to try—it just means that garlic doesn't make my surefire list for Florida.

Grain Corn

Grain corn is perhaps a little easier than sweet corn but requires a lot of feeding. It's worth it if you want grits, but it's not ever going to be a great yielder compared to the space it takes up. The best harvests I've gotten are from Hickory King and Tex Cuban, though Tex Cuban was a pretty tasteless corn. I refuse to grow the genetically modified monsters developed by laboratories; I stick with heirlooms only.

Jerusalem Artichoke

Up north, Jerusalem artichokes are super-easy to grow. Down here they tend to have rot issues, never get all that big, and have trouble dealing with the heat and the warm winters. When you do get a harvest and eat them, they'll give you gas like you wouldn't believe. You'll have an overwhelming urge to stab your stomach with a skewer to make the pain stop. No lie.

Watermelons

Little watermelons usually do better for me than big ones. My best luck has been planting them in melon pits (get my book Compost Everything: The Good Guide to Extreme Composting to read more about melon pits) and taking whatever yields I get. My best melons usually get wrecked by raccoons or rot issues.

Onions

Onions are worth planting for their greens, but don't expect to have easy success getting them to set big bulbs. They often grow to about half the size they should be, then die back or rot.

Peas

Peas yield too little to be worth much, though I often plant beds of them just to add nitrogen to the soil and for the children to pick. They're not hard if you plant them during the cool season, but they're not all that efficient either.

Potatoes

I've discovered an inconvenient truth about Florida and potatoes: fire ants love to chew up potato roots. They'll get into your potato patch and nest all around the base of the plants, utterly ruining your harvests and wrecking the plants' productivity. Grow yams instead.

Sweet Corn

Sweet corn may be worth growing as a nice vegetable, but I wouldn't count on it for much of my diet.

Touchy and/or Low-Yielding Vegetables

Sweet peppers

Bell peppers are a much-loved vegetable that's also somewhat difficult to grow successfully. They like rich soil, and they tend to get nailed by various rot issues and insects. Yields have always been poor for us. Unless you want to baby them, don't bother.

Tomatoes (except the Everglades tomato)

Tomatoes are the one vegetable everyone wants to grow yet finds completely frustrating. See more in Appendix IV. Not recommended for beginners or people interested in low-work yields.

Yacon

I got excited about trying yacon a few years ago but have since discovered it doesn't like the heat and needs consistent moisture to bear a yield. The roots taste sweet and crisp if you can get them to set... but I don't think they're worth the effort.

If you're a beginning Florida gardener or someone interested in gardening as a way to grow a lot of food, I recommend leaving the touchy vegetables for later—unless you just feel like you have to try.

I would never say don't grow them, but I will say this: if you build your main gardens from the plants on the easy list, you'll bring in more food for less work. Try the harder plants after you're feeding yourself well on the first group. For those of you who are saying "But hey—I grew eggplant, and it made basketfuls... it was so easy!" or "I know this way of growing tomatoes that...", don't get on my case too much. I know that there are times when stuff just does well; however, after three decades of Florida gardening and lots of experience with new gardeners, I don't want to give anyone false expectations.

Yes—all those crops can be grown and can sometimes be very productive; it's just that they're not totally crazy easy like the stuff on my main crop list. It's not wrong to plant them and, as you get better as a gardener, I'm sure you'll want to grow some of those things.

If you're a beginner, though—just start with the really easy stuff and move on from there.

Chapter 7

PEST CONTROL OR: HOW I LEARNED TO STOP WORRYING AND LOVE THE BUGS

What is our obsession with killing insects?

I was once in the garden section at Home Depot, talking with an employee who knew I was (at that point) a Florida Master Gardener. As we were chatting, a man walked up and started looking through the pesticides near us. He looked a bit confused, so the Home Depot worker asked him if he needed help.

"I want to kill the (insert name of pest here) in my grass," he stated. "What would work for that?"

"I'm sure we have something that will work," she replied to the customer, then gestured at me, "you should ask David—he's a Master Gardener."

The man turned to me with a couple of jugs of poison in his hands. "Which of these would kill them?"

I took the bottles and read the labels. Both were indeed toxic. Both would very much kill a wide range of insect life.

I handed them back to the man. "You know, I wouldn't spray anything."

"What? Why not?" he asked.

"Because you'll end up killing all kinds of good insects along with the bad ones."

"Hmph," he responded, then looked at the jug in his right hand, "says here this one also kills fleas."

"Do you have fleas in your yard?" I asked.

"No."

"Then why do you need a poison to kill them?"

"I might have fleas at some point," he stated, then shuffled off with his insect WMD.

I was frustrated. Most people simply don't see the intricate web of life that fills the environment—even in an ecosystem as barren as a front lawn.

Spraying poison to kill a pest is like adjusting a Swiss watch with a sledgehammer. Not only does it kill the "bad" bugs, it kills a lot more—plus it poisons your living space and maybe even our water supply.

I haven't had to spray anything more toxic than homemade sprays in over a decade. The only pesticide I do use—in moderation and with resignation—is Amdro™ fire ant bait. Even then I only use it when the ant piles get ridiculous and the children are in danger playing outdoors. Fire ants are an imported non-native species here that doesn't fit into the environment; that means they are without natural predators.

For most other insect problems, the cure is already built into the environment.

The lure of pesticides for most gardeners is twofold:

1. We don't like to see anything attack our plants.

When you've nurtured something up from a little seed or transplant, lovingly watered, fertilized, and cared for that plant… then you see insects chewing away at it, there's a sense of violation. *"How dare they!"*

Here's the real scoop: many insect attacks don't kill the host plants. A few bug bites in your cabbages, beans, etc. can be shrugged off by the plant. Major infestations cannot. Most insect damage consists of drive-by attacks, not full-on assaults. Be calm. If you spray, you're poisoning your food. Leave that madness to industrial agriculture… as for me, I prefer my salads non-toxic with a few bug bites.

2. We control our land with a heavy hand.

This obviously ties in with the first point about not letting minor bug damage get to you, but it goes further than that.

The desire for order runs deep. For some reason, it seems to run even deeper in gardeners. We need to make our plants behave! Nature must submit! Insects must flee from our wrath!

Yet the ecosystem is a self-balancing affair when it's healthy. "Healthy" doesn't look like straight rows of one crop; "healthy" is more like a forest edge. A rich diversity of plants makes for a rich diversity of both pests and predators.

Agricultural experiments have shown that leaving un-mown hedgerows or "nature strips" (or whatever they're called right now) along the edges of plowed fields greatly reduces the need for pesticide application. Why? Because predators have a place to live.

If you don't spray at all, leave lots of creature habitat around your gardens and mix up species, many of your pest problems will melt away.

An additional benefit, at least in my mind, is that my family gets to see a wide range of insects, some of which are rarely seen in most yards. Leaving habitat and not spraying make for interesting bug-catching. We've seen insects such as the big-eyed elater beetle, a marvelous array of dragonflies, twice-stabbed lady beetles, bright orange and black milkweed bugs, luna moths, various scarab beetles, and a lot more. Many of these insects wouldn't be here if we sprayed our gardens.

Resist the urge to call down chemical vengeance on your garden's enemies unless you're dealing with a serious problem on an expensive perennial.

Going without spraying is better for the good bugs, better for the environment, and better for you.

But... if you don't spray poisons... how *do* you control pests?

I'm glad you asked. Here are four ways you can deal with pests naturally and make your yard and garden a nicer place to live.

1. Make space for bees and wasps.

So, you've planted your garden at a good time in the spring. Everything looks good right now... but like it or not, caterpillars and other bad guys are going to show up eventually and try to eat all your hard work.

Did you know that wasps are one of the major predators of caterpillars? I know—you're thinking "I *hate* wasps!" or "my baby lemur is *sooooo* allergic!"

Okay, I know. Wasps aren't all that likeable... until you realize that they spend a lot of their waking lives patrolling your garden, looking for caterpillars and grasshoppers they can kill and feed to their babies.

I've noticed that wasps have a tendency to build nests in my mailbox. After seeing that happen multiple times, I thought,

"Hey, why not put a row of mailboxes above my garden in which the wasps can build their nests?"

I also took pieces of dry wood and drilled a bunch of various sized holes into them that were at least 4 inches deep. I then bundled them with small pieces of hollow bamboo, all holes facing outwards, into a wine box and hung it from the garden fence with an old baking tray tacked on top to keep the rain out. It was rapidly colonized by a variety of solitary bees and wasps, some of which hunt insects in my garden. Many of them also pollinate my vegetables and fruits.

One year I watched some sort of solitary bee shoving paralyzed or dead stinkbugs into the pipes of the wind chime on my back porch. Bees and wasps are good guys. You may not have to build places for them to live, but by all means—quit spraying their nests! Our caterpillar populations have dropped, and yours will too.

2. Leave space for other good guys... and their prey.

When we rip out a bed of spent tomatoes or chop down the rest of the season's weed-infested collards, what happens to the ladybugs, wheelbugs, assassin bugs and other good guys that moved in over the summer? They fly off in search of greener pastures. That's not to say you should leave tons of rotting vegetable plants everywhere; it just means you should think twice before you clear everything from your beds or cut down all the weeds. I deliberately leave patches of weeds here and there around my yard and gardens for beneficial insects to live in. I also plant perennial garden beds in between my annual beds and include lots of insectary plants like African blue basil, milkweed, and various bloomers like pentas and flowering almond.

Though it sounds counter-intuitive, you should actually *want* places for aphids and pests to live. Having some aphids around draws in the ladybugs and increases their population. By letting patches of plants sit, you create habitats—and ladybugs aren't the only creatures that will benefit. You'll also be creating space for praying mantises, lacewings, wheelbugs, lizards, frogs, toads, centipedes, spiders, worms, and pollinators like moths, butterflies, bees, and wasps.

Beyond leaving weeds and spent plants around, you can also add rock piles, logs, stacks of sticks, and water sources to your gardens.

3. Intercrop and rotate.

Intercropping is one of the best things you can do to lower pest problems and preserve the soil in your garden or food forest.

Pest Control or: How I Learned to Stop Worrying and...

God is said to be a God of order... so if that's the case, why does nature look like a rambling mess of vines, scraggly sumacs, tumbling-down oaks, and a profusion of annual weeds?

It's because the order is a lot more complex than we realize. Generally, human beings like geometric forms and straight lines. We like to see all our corn in neat rows and our grapes on taut lines. And when it comes to harvesting and planting, there is an ease to this system.

In Florida, however, some of those neat rows more closely resemble a death march across the desert than a good food source. We're always watering the thirsty sand, picking off lubbers or aphids, and praying things will live long enough to produce.

When you add more species, however, things change. You're no longer counting on one thing to produce heavily enough to justify its existence. You're also not trusting that patch of earth to be the Perfect Lil' Environment™ for whatever you're craving. Instead, you're making a mix of plants—and often their interactions allow a greater harvest across that patch than would be possible alone. The benefits of putting marigolds in your garden has been expounded at length—we've all heard that they repel pests. In reality, they don't seem to make much difference; yet the more plants you put together, the more pests seem to be confused by the profusion.

Many pests are host-specific, which means they only like to eat certain plants. Mix up the menu with plants they can't eat—or ones that might even be toxic to them—and your garden goes from being a bug buffet to an outlet condemned by the Stinkbug Health Department.

Herbs, flowers, beans, greens, climbers, creepers, and shrubs all have their place in a home garden. Mix them up, and you'll mix up the pests, too.

What intercropping will help you do:

1. Confuse pests
2. Build the soil
3. Harvest a wider variety of plants
4. Conserve space
5. Freak out neatniks
6. Keep moisture in the soil
7. Ensure you harvest something

Pretty good list, eh?

Nature is a big mess of different things growing together. Do the same in your garden, and you'll profit from the design God has thoughtfully laid out for us.

4. Be vigilant.

One of the biggest keys to having a successful garden is just being there.

Walk around your garden regularly. Talk to your plants. Sing. Look for yellow leaves and water stress. Deadhead the marigolds, pick the ripe tomatoes… and always watch for the bad guys.

I talked to a friend while writing this book and he told me that he had great-looking tomato plants that were as tall as he was… until he went out of town on a business trip.

His wife checked the garden after a couple of days, only to find the tomato plants were completely stripped of leaves and blooms… and on them, were thirteen big, fat, ugly, and quite happy tomato hornworms.

If you walk around regularly and keep your eyes on your garden, you're going to have a successful garden. Plant your garden where you'll see it... not at the edge of the yard... and you've already won half the battle.

A lot of the really irritating pests arise because gardens get planted too late in the year. You may not be able to get rid of stink bugs and leaf-footed bugs easily, but there are certainly a lot less of them in the spring than there are in the summer. Plant at the right times and life will be a lot easier.

If you see them, you can also just pick them or knock them off your plants. I'll take a bowl of water with a few drops of dishwashing liquid in it to break the surface tension (this causes insects to drown rapidly) and wander around the garden regularly, knocking pest insects into it and cackling. You can do this too. The cackling is optional but I find it helps.

Conclusion

Your Florida gardening doesn't have to be a failure. It doesn't even have to be particularly hard.

If you take anything away from this book, let it be this: Plant the crops that are totally crazy easy to grow in Florida and the rest is a piece of cake.

To find new totally crazy easy crops for Florida, I recommend making friends with gardeners from India, Thailand, Malaysia, Jamaica, Congo, and other tropical countries and see what they're growing. Ethnic markets are a good place to find interesting tropical fruits, vegetables, and seeds you can grow. Did you see a really cool calabaza squash with a sticker reading "origin: Honduras?" Grab it, eat it, then plant the seeds!

Experiment constantly. Once you get the hang of growing a few great solid crops, move on from there.

Totally crazy easy Florida gardening can be yours. You just need to get out there, find the right plants, then get planting!

Appendix I

RECOMMENDED FLORIDA GARDENING BOOKS

Here are a few of the best books for Florida Gardeners:

Create Your Own Florida Food Forest by David The Good

Yes, I wrote this short book. And it's great. Just the "cheat sheet for Florida gardeners" you'll find in Appendix 3 is worth the tiny price of the book.

How to Grow More Vegetables, Eighth Edition by John Jeavons

This is a great jump into biointensive gardening. It relies on little to no external inputs and gives you excellent results, even in sand.

Gardening Without Irrigation

On the other side of the spectrum from Jeavons' intensive beds is Steve Solomon's approach to wide row gardening in low rain conditions. This is how I grow my corn and other field crops without having to water. Go to the free download page of Project Gutenberg. Don't bother buying this book—it's public domain.

Gardening When It Counts: Growing Food in Hard Times

Another Steve Solomon epic. Contains a lot of good information and thoughts on feeding yourself under adverse conditions. A must-have.

Gaia's Garden: A Guide to Home-Scale Permaculture, 2nd Edition

Fruitcake name but killer information. This will transform the way you look at food growing, gardening, and the ecosystem around your house.

Perennial Vegetables: From Artichokes to Zuiki Taro, A Gardener's Guide to Over 100 Delicious and Easy to Grow Edibles

Toensmeier's classic look at veggies you *only have to plant once.* Many of the selections are perfect for Florida; in fact, reading this book is likely to make temperate gardeners cry.

Compost Everything: The Good Guide to Extreme Composting

This is my survival manual for feeding your gardens in a collapse without outside inputs, cleverly disguised as a hilarious book on composting. If you want to compost easily and grow the best gardens for the least amount of work and inputs, buy it. You'll like it.

I recommend any gardener read these. I look at buying physical copies of great gardening books as part of my insurance plan for the future. If things collapse, I'll still have my books and the knowledge therein. What may seem like a big purchase now may look dirt cheap in the future when you really need to get some food on the table.

Load up your Amazon cart and buy them when you get a chance, then spend a month reading. It's worth it.

Appendix II

PERENNIAL AND FOREST GARDENING IN FLORIDA

Ever leave your yard alone for a few weeks? Or a few months? Or a few years?

The smoking remains of the housing market have given us some insight into what happens to a lawn when folks lose their over-mortgaged "pride of ownership" and leave their underwater houses for friendlier shores.

First, the grass grows long and sends up seed heads. Opportunistic weeds start to appear. Vines grow over the fence. Buried acorns sprout. Black cherry and wild plum pits dropped by powerline-straddling birds germinate amidst the unraked oak and magnolia leaves. I have a friend who picks loads of berries from a local "blackberry patch," which just so happens to be the front yard of a neighboring house abandoned in the ongoing real estate bust.

As soon as our management ends, complex biological webs begin their assault on imposed order and HOA regulations. A lawn—however lovely and enjoyable—is a very low-level ecological system. Nothing stands still for very long in nature. If you take a look around our area, you'll see that mature ecosystems in our area are generally oak or pine forests. But of course—they're not just oaks or pines. They also host cabbage palms, passion vines, palmettos, wild grapes, mimosas, hickories, coral beans, sumacs, beautyberries, and a wide variety of other species. Does your yard do the same? Only if you leave it alone... and sometimes the results aren't pretty for a long, long time. Dog fennel, anyone?

Maintaining grass is tough. Especially when you try to do so around trees and islands of ornamentals. You'll almost never see trees naturally growing alone in a field of grass... except in the African savannah. And there they have frequent wildfires and grazing animals that keep forests from forming. Here we generally have lawnmowers and weedeaters. You have to slave at your yard work because you're trying to maintain something that doesn't want to stay where it is.

Now... there's an opportunity in here, if you choose to run with it. What if you created a forest ecosystem piece by piece? But rather than letting birds and squirrels start it—you plant it. If you choose the right species, you can make an Eden of food... an oasis of drifting butterflies... a lush jungle of green; you're only limited by your location and imagination. The more species you add, the more ecological niches you're creating. Different plants attract different insects, birds, and other friendly creatures. And with a wide variety of organisms, it's hard for pest or disease problems to destroy your system. Predators have hiding places and species-specific pests like aphids can't jump plant to plant as easily. Chinch bugs can wipe out a St. Augustine lawn. Frost can wreck a citrus grove. Drought can ruin a wheat field. But if you're growing dozens or even hundreds of different species, the chances of the system failing are almost zero.

Rather than a monoculture of grass, you're going to create an ecological web. When this kind of system is created for edible purposes, it's usually called a "food forest" or "forest gardening." English horticulturist Robert Hart is probably most responsible for the modern interest in edible landscaping and forest creation. He took a tiny orchard and filled it with edible perennial species, stacking herbs, vegetables and berries into every corner until the system matured into an amazing food-creating machine. His work has since been improved upon and expanded by permaculturists such as Bill Mollison and Geoff Lawton (look these guys up… it'll blow your mind).

Here in Florida, we've got a big advantage over Robert Hart: we have very mild winters. That means we get to choose from a huge range of edible and useful species. If you've ever been to Kanapaha Botanical Gardens in Gainesville or Fairchild Tropical Gardens in Coral Gables, you know what I mean. The sheer variety is overwhelming. And in terms of work, forest gardening beats annual beds hands down. Think about how much work it takes to weed, hoe, till, plant, spray and harvest a garden. Talk about labor! Now think about how easy it is to pick up grapefruit or pecans from beneath a mature tree. When a tree gets big enough to take care of itself, it becomes a long-term producer of food… without all the murderous work.

Now you may be looking at your grass and saying "where in the world would I start?" Start small—but not too small. Get yourself a handful of fruit trees and some edible shrubs and perennials. Tear out some grass and plant a little orchard with the trees. Then surround those with shrubs—and surround the shrubs with small perennials. Mulch and water heavily, and try to keep the grass out until the shade system does the job for you. Don't throw away leaves, twigs, and grass clippings! Drop them right around your new plants as they become available—covering our sand is very important for the soil's health and fertility.

What you're doing here should look a lot like a little chunk of woods. If you have more space, start with some great big trees, like pecans, in the middle. Then surround those with persimmons, pomegranates, loquats, mulberry trees, figs, chestnuts, pears and other fruit trees that thrive here. For the shrubs, think of things like cassava, blueberries (dig in some rotted pine bark or peat when you plant them), thornless blackberries, prickly pears, cattley guavas, Simpson stoppers (they're native *and* edible!), goumi berries (they taste like cherries and fix nitrogen in the soil), sugarcane, beautyberries (yes, they're edible!), etc. Then around those, add in native plants, edibles, and herbs. Things like coral bean (not edible but it attracts pollinators), aloes, sage, coneflowers, lemongrass, rosemary, canna lilies (the flowers and roots are edible), wormwood, and passionvines.

Remember: this is a long-term forest you're making. The first few years are going to require watering, feeding, trimming, and weeding. Some pieces won't survive. But then... magic happens. The forest begins to take over... and soon you have a garden you can pass on to your children's children—which isn't something you can say for the weed patch left after summer's corn harvest.

So... what are you waiting for? Get your hands in the dirt and start learning. Walk around in the woods and look at how trees and plants interact. Start spotting the different layers of a forest and see how all the spots are filled. And, of course... I have to say it: pick up a copy of my book *Create Your Own Florida Food Forest* for plenty more inspiration and lists of species that do great in Florida. It's $2.99 and it will save you lots of energy in the long run... plus, once your yard is an Eden... that 2.99 will look like the best three bucks you ever spent.

Appendix III

GROWING SUGARCANE

There's nothing like whittling off a hunk of sugarcane stem with your pocketknife and enjoying that sweet juice on a hot day.

I remember a friend bringing over a cane to share when I was a boy. It was like magic tasting this big hunk of bamboo-like grass filled with amazing flavor.

People have this idea that sugarcane is something that requires year-round tropical weather and a big old swamp. Fortunately, that idea is wrong. You can grow sugarcane successfully all the way up into Georgia and probably beyond, swamp or no swamp.

Other than its delicious flavor, sugarcane is also attractive as an ornamental. Depending on the variety, the thick canes can range in color from dark red-brown to yellow-green and have a very similar appearance to bamboo in the landscape. Since it's a perennial plant, once you plant sugarcane you can look forward to having it for years.

The hardest part about growing sugarcane might be finding the plants in the first place. I've never seen it for sale at a plant nursery. Ask for sugarcane, and you're likely to get a blank look and the question "does that even grow here?"

It's okay that they don't have any—you really don't need to buy a potted sugarcane plant. All you need is a good hunk of sugarcane with a couple of intact nodes (those are the joints in the cane). Since sugarcane is usually harvested in the fall, that's the time you're likely to see the canes for sale. Most grocery stores don't carry sugarcane, but a lot of farm stands do in the fall—and fall is when you want to plant. I drove down 441 in Central Florida one afternoon a few years ago and bought two different varieties of sugarcane from two different produce vendors located only a few miles apart. Grab a couple of stout canes (they're usually 5–6 feet long with about 8–12 nodes, depending on the cultivar), and you're well on your way.

When you get home, cut your canes into segments with at least 3–4 nodes each, pick a good spot to plant them, then put those pieces on their sides about 4–6 inches down, and cover them up well.

This is the second hardest part about growing sugarcane. Waiting for them to pop up.

All winter, those pieces will sit down there in the ground until the soil warms up in the spring. You'll think they're dead... you'll forget about them... you'll start building a gazebo in the spot where they were buried... you'll get married and give up on the gazebo... move away to Los Vegas... start a family... launch an online business... buy a bass boat... sell a bass boat... visit Area 51 and have your camera confiscated after you photograph something interesting... invest in a condo development... file for bankruptcy... discover your spouse is a werewolf... get moved back to your old house in a bizarre failure of the Lycanthropic Witness Protection Program... and then, one day, you'll be in the backyard, see the sugarcane poking out of the ground amidst the rotted pieces of that gazebo you never finished and think, "What the heck? Is this bamboo?"

Actually, that was a slight exaggeration. When I plant sugarcane in November, the plants always pop up for me sometime in March or April. For each cane you bury, you'll usually get a couple of good shoots emerging from the ground.

If you really don't want to trust the earth to take care of your little baby sugarcane plants, you can just stick some chunks of cane in pots with a node or two beneath the dirt and keep them someplace that doesn't freeze, like a sunroom. They'll grow.

When my baby sugarcane plants appear in the spring—and I'm pretty sure it's not going to freeze again—I fertilize them with chicken manure. You can also use lawn fertilizer. (They're a grass—they like lots of nitrogen.) Throughout the summer they'll get nice and tall and sometime in July or August you'll really see the canes starting to thicken up, but don't chop them yet (unless you really can't stand to wait). Wait until it's just about time for the first frost of fall or winter, then go cut the canes down—that way you'll get the largest harvest possible.

If you don't cut them down and you get a freeze, you're going to lose all the above ground growth and you may even lose the plants. Harvest by cutting the canes down close to the ground, and then put the sugarcane roots to bed for the winter by mulching over them with some rough material. Leaves are good for this, but probably any mulch would work fine. My sugarcane came back even when I barely mulched over the roots.

In its second year, sugarcane will bunch out and hopefully give you a few more canes than it did the first year… which means you'll be able to share the abundance. Heck, you might even be able to make your own molasses. Or just sell the canes you don't want and buy molasses at the store. Along with a pre-made gazebo. And maybe a new camera.

Appendix IV

Growing Tomatoes in Florida

If there's a Holy Grail of vegetable gardening... it has to be the tomato.

Armies of fervent gardeners fight to grow this succulent fruit. Seed catalogs devote multiple pages to exotic varieties ranging from black-fleshed beefsteaks to tart yellow Romas. Home improvement stores roll out racks of rich green young seedlings in perfect six-packs...

Yet, tomatoes are not for me. Here I am... a garden teacher... writer... genius. And a failure at tomatoes. At least in this climate.

From the fringe of outer darkness I stare inward, picturing happy gardeners picking supple fruits hanging in golden sunshine; lush tomatoes, untouched by stinkbugs... plump and sweet without a hint of blossom end rot...

The temptation to try again is overwhelming.

But... the pain... oh... the pain.
Ave Solanum, Solanum lycopersicum...

It wasn't always like this, you know.

There was a year when tomatoes grew well for me... unfortunately, I was in Tennessee at the time. Tomatoes loved the rich clay and deep mulch of my beds (though they still rejected much of my trellising efforts, preferring to twine about on the ground like overzealous revelers ejected from a Bacchanal) and rewarded me for my efforts by producing enough fruit for us to eat fresh and even jar up some homemade tomato sauce on the side.

Sadly for my tomato-growing career, now I live in North Florida... and have proven again and again that gardening methods that work in one place don't necessarily carry over to another.

But... wait a minute!

I do have one friend who grows great tomatoes down here. And if you're dealing with tomato issues, I bet her advice might help you as well.

My friend? Her name is Jo. She's a Master Gardener and an organic grower.

You know what? I think I'll stop griping about tomatoes and give her a ring.

(David scrambles through his address book... picks up the phone... then dials.)

Ring...

Ring...

Rin—click

Jo: Hello?

David: Hi Jo. It's David. I'm writing something on how I can't grow tomatoes here and I'm whining about how it's impossible... then I realized that you do it every year... so... I need to know... how *do* you grow tomatoes?

Jo: First, I grow varieties that are suited to the climate. Better Boy, Early Girl, Roma, and Amish Paste do well.

David: How do you start them?

Jo: In January, I start them from seed in the greenhouse, then transplant them to the garden on Feb 14th. [*Note:* your local planting and pre-planting times may vary from Jo's USDA zone 8b/9a climate. Check with your local extension office for frost-free dates]. When I transplant, I always bury half the little tomato plant's stem in the soil so it builds extra roots. Then I put a ring of paper around the base of each plant to protect them from cutworms. Just use brown paper grocery bags. If it's going to freeze, I protect them with cloches. I just use milk jugs with the bottoms cut off.

David: I'm convinced that seed-grown plants are tougher than transplants you get from the store. It makes sense to get them started early, too, and let them adapt to your garden. What do you do about feeding them?

Jo: I use composted cow manure, mushroom compost, bone meal, blood meal, eggshells, and ashes for potassium. After things warm up a bit and I don't need the cloches, I put cages around each plant and mulch with 4–6 inches of straw.

David: I think my problem is that I'm starting too late here…

Jo: Yes, you need to start early and get as much harvest in as possible before the bugs arrive.

David: Anything else I should know?

Jo: Well, people often ask when I give talks, "So, I have these tomato plants that look great but they aren't blooming or setting fruit… why is that?" Usually, it's because they're getting too much nitrogen and not enough phosphorus and potassium. High nitrogen isn't a good idea… if you don't go organic, you gotta watch that first number if you're using chemical fertilizer.

David: Another thing I've noticed: tomatoes in part shade won't fruit.

Jo: That's right. Full sun means six hours. If they don't get that, then no tomatoes!

David: Thanks, Jo. Now I can at least share a little hope with my readers...

Jo: Any time.

So there you have it. It *is*, apparently, possible to grow great tomatoes, even in Florida... It just takes planning and a lot of work. It also doesn't hurt to have at least two green thumbs... like Jo.

Appendix V

FIVE CROPS THAT HANDLE SUMMER HEAT

One steamy day in early June I walked past one of my spring garden beds in the heat of the early afternoon. The once-proud carrots were having a really bad hair day, the cabbages were one step from the guillotine, and the row of purple kohlrabi looked significantly less royal than usual.

I've already told you that one of the great things about Florida is that you can "garden year-round," but if you talk to most Florida gardeners, you'll find they only believe in two growing seasons: spring and fall.

Despite the heat-induced siesta many of us take, and though it's not easy to grow in summer, you can do it if you choose the right plants.

But... what do you plant? It's too danged hot for most food plants in the summer—and there's a good reason for that. As I've written previously, most of our common garden vegetables were bred for temperate climates. In order to have success, you need to dip into the glorious tropics for species that can handle the heat.

SWEET POTATOES

Probably the tastiest summer crop is the sweet potato. It's not too late to plant them in June, though you might have a hard time finding slips ("slips" are what they call baby sweet potato plants) at your local nursery or garden center. If you don't have luck, buy some good-looking sweet potatoes from your local grocery store and plant them about 4 feet from each other in a prepared bed. I plant them in my garden beds as I yank out spring crops. June is stretching the season, but you should be fine… unless the theories of a new Ice Age are true and we end up getting a frost in October. I've grown sweet potatoes in my blueberry patch, around trees, in double-dug beds, in square foot gardens and in my wife's rose garden. They're really easy. Water them for the first few weeks and then stand back.

Okra

Another crop that will handle the heat is okra! Yeah, I know, it's slimy, but hey, it grows in the summer. (You can't say that about heirloom rutabagas, can you? Can you?) Okra will handle tons of heat, just don't plant it where you planted okra in a previous year. They're nematode magnets—in fact, the University of Florida uses okra in its nematode control experiments, just because it's such a tasty plant for these oh-so-irritating psuedocoelomates. You can plant okra all the way through June—they're tough, heat-loving and easy to grow (if not easy to eat).

Cassava

Though it's not easy to find, cassava is a major staple in many equatorial nations. If you plant it in summer it won't make big roots until the following year, but it'll thrive during the hot rainy days and be in great shape for next year's fall harvest. This is a long-term perennial plant, with graceful 12-foot canes and swaying palmate leaves. It will usually freeze to the ground during the winter—but don't worry, it'll come back. I've planted them from spring to fall, had good success rates, and eaten plenty of delicious fried roots over the years. This plant is basically pest and maintenance-free… as long as you don't mind the wait. (Remember to cook it right, or it'll kill you. Don't be scared—just look it up online.)

Snake Beans

Moving away from roots and slimy things, our third summer garden candidate is one of my personal favorites: the snake bean! This crop is unbeatable for this region. The 18-inch pods make great green beans and don't need shelling. As a bonus, the plant grows in poor soil, in half-shade, in full sun, in , and in the gardens of people who can't grow anything else. Make sure you plant them next to a chain-link fence or a strong trellis; the vines will grow quite tall and can knock down weak supports. Pick when the pods are about 14 inches long, and they won't be as stringy. Keep harvesting regularly, and they'll produce more for you—and that's saying a lot, since this plant is very prolific.

A Final Thought

So—are you encouraged yet? It's hard to work in the heat—but with good plants that will do some of the work for you, you can still stay fed on good stuff despite the blazing sun.

Acknowledgments

This book is the result of years of gardening, experimenting, testing, writing, blogging, cooking, and making do on a tight budget with a growing family to feed. Thanks are due to quite a few folks.

First of all, I thank my parents for encouraging me in my gardening efforts as a child.

I'd also like to thank Chet and Dave Womach at ThePrepperProject.com for pushing me to write and to research gardening topics I hadn't previously covered and for graciously allowing me to reuse portions of my columns in this book.

Thanks also to:

Rick Morris for help with the technical issues on my website and the ongoing encouragement to write.

Mart Hale for all the crazy ideas and fellow plant geekiness

Craig Hepworth for the recommendation to test and grow yams

Jeanne Logue for her excellent editing and proofreading

Jo Leyte-Vidal for allowing me to interview her on how she grows tomatoes

Andy and Lynn Greene for the use of their field for test crops

Jake Sims for gardening advice and for tilling my plots with his tractor

Jeff Greene for videography and helping tweak my YouTube channel (subscribe at youtube.com/user/davidthegood)

Acknowledgments

Cathy Bowers for the encouragement, first aid, and help in the food forest

Allen Dovico for getting me plants I couldn't find

Dave and Guda Taylor for letting me borrow space in the Taylor Gardens Nursery (taylorgardensnursery.com) greenhouse for my propagation experiments

Fred O'Brien for donating his old mailboxes to me as wasp houses

John Crawford for pushing me to think big

Andi Houston for being a fellow mad gardener and source of inspiration

Cathy Snyder for giving me space at the great little 326 Market

Carolyn Blakeslee for getting me started as a garden writer by publishing my columns for almost two years in *Natural Awakenings* magazine

Kevan Chandler for telling me to migrate my gardening blog from a crummy setup to one that worked

Paul Wheaton for creating permies.com so I had other nutty gardeners with whom to converse

My children for letting me put off everything to write

My wife, Rachel, for figuring out how to cook the crazy plants I grow

ABOUT THE AUTHOR

David The Good is a naturalist, part-time scientist, and hard-core gardener who has grown his own food since 1984. In Kindergarten he sprouted a bean in a Dixie cup of soil and hasn't stopped growing since.

David is the author of three more books; *Survival Gardening Secrets, Create Your Own Florida Food Forest* and his latest Amazon best seller, *Compost Everything: The Good Guide to Extreme Composting.* He's also the creator of the popular gardening film 13 *Tips, Tricks and Lessons from Homesteading an Acre.* Subscribe to his YouTube channel at http://www.youtube.com/user/davidthegood.

David currently has over 20 intensive beds, over 100 fruit trees, and a series of ongoing experiments in progress, ranging from cross-species grafting to breeding a better tropical pumpkin. He currently lives somewhere in the tropics with his wife Rachel and their clan of young gardeners.

Sign up for great gardening ideas and exclusive content here: http://eepurl.com/buoMKL.

More of David's ongoing experiments can be found at his website www.thesurvivalgardener.com.

Made in the USA
Columbia, SC
01 January 2023